ROOTS AND WINGS

ROOTS
AND WINGS

The human journey from a speck of stardust
to a spark of God

MARGARET SILF

NOVALIS

Published in Canada by Novalis
Business Offices:
Novalis Publishing Inc.
10 Lower Spadina Avenue, Suite 400
Toronto, Ontario, Canada
M5V 2Z2

Novalis Publishing Inc.
4475 Frontenac Street
Montréal, Québec, Canada
H2H 2S2

Phone: 1-800-387-7164
Fax: 1-800-204-4140
E-mail: books@novalis.ca
www.novalis.ca

ISBN 10: 2-89507-825-4
ISBN 13: 978-2-89507-825-8

Cataloguing in Publication is available from Library and Archives Canada

Printed and Bound in Great Britain

Contents

Prologue

In the beginning is a 'singularity', smaller than a grain of salt, beyond which the mind of neither scientist nor theologian can penetrate. This is the source of our universe and ourselves. But what of our destiny? Does the speck of stardust that is our origin also hold within it a 'spark of God'? Could it be evolving to levels of consciousness that we cannot begin, as yet, even to imagine?

Exploring the story of the tree of life, and the particular branch of that tree that we call humanity, opens up far more questions than answers. The quest to understand who we are, where we come from and where we are going entices us to put a toe into the ocean of that mystery even though, if we are honest, we know that the little we think we know merely points us to the vast tracts of all we *don't* know, and maybe can never fully know and understand.

And in the beginning of a book that invites the reader to explore nothing less than the universe story, I am especially aware of my profound ignorance, being neither a scientist nor a theologian. Yet, like many millions of my fellow human beings I am fascinated, and indeed awed, by the story of how human life is unfolding – a story that is increasingly accessible to the lay person through non-specialist books, TV documentaries and the internet.

So I find myself fired by the wonders that science is revealing, as well as being deeply inspired by the wisdom of the spiritual traditions of the human family. Holding the empirical evidence of science and the intuited wisdom of spirituality together in one mind and heart isn't always easy and yet I feel that this challenge points to a necessary paradox, a creative tension which we must embrace, if we are to evolve further into the great adventure of becoming fully human. Faith that flies in the face of empirical evidence is a belief system built on sand, and facts that deny the validity of numinous experience and a sense of the otherness of the mystery seem to me to be equally incomplete.

Roots and Wings is a kind of 'toe-print' into these waters where science meets spirituality and mind makes room for heart. It's my own toe-print, and it reflects and explores some of the big questions that are around for me. It makes no claim to provide any answers, nor does it presume to predict what *your* big questions may be. What it does do, though, is to

insist that the big questions can and may be asked, even though they may
upset a few apple-carts among those who believe we have got the story
all sewn up.

It is also my belief that evolution is going somewhere, not just physically, but also spiritually, and this process may be much more than the
passive unfolding of some blueprint written in the heavens or the genes.
It may actually be a destiny we ourselves are shaping and co-creating in
the way we choose to live and relate to each other and our earth. It is in
our power, in so many ways, to foster what is making us more fully
human and work against what is tending to de-humanise us.

In her book *Turning to One Another*, Margaret Wheatley reminds us that
'real change begins with the simple act of people talking about what they
care about.' So my hope for this book is that it might be something of a
'conversation starter', a catalyst for a wider debate about what it really
means to be a human *and* a spiritual being in a world that at present finds
itself so dangerously polarised.

It has been wisely said that we approach the core of each other most
truly when we travel down through the roots of our own spiritual traditions. This book grows from the roots of the Judeo-Christian tradition
and a big question for me is what the life of Jesus of Nazareth means in
the context of a universe story that extends back for fifteen billion years.
If this is a big question for you too, I hope this book might help you to
discover your own authentic answers.

However, my hunch is that when we finally touch the core of what it
means to be fully and truly human, we will eventually realise that our
various spiritual traditions, at their best, have been the carriers of a dream
that will one day be able to shed its chrysalis and fly free of all limiting
and divisive structures and doctrines. Meanwhile, as we each walk the way
of our own tradition or personal spiritual conviction, let us seek to do so
with open eyes, open minds and open hearts. And we might fruitfully
share in lively conversation with each other as we walk, without feeling
obliged either to agree with, or to convert each other.

During recent years I have had the joy and the privilege of meeting
thousands of people who are asking their own questions and holding
conversations of this nature. I thank them all for the inspiration and
encouragement they have given me personally. My special thanks go to:
Jane Besly, Joyce Campbell, Maura Dillon, Anna Garvie, Mary Griffiths,
Gerard Hughes, Marion Jepson, Enid Nussbaum, Helen Porter, Kath
Saltwell and Brendan Walsh for their kindness and patience in reading and
commenting on the manuscript, and to those who have joined with me
in exploring 'God's Unfinished Story' in retreats and days of reflection.

Alan Turing once said: 'Science is a differential equation. Religion is a boundary condition.' It seems to me completely reasonable to admire and trust the elegance and truth that the differential equation expresses and reveals, while continuing to live and grow in the mystery of the boundary condition. But you must decide for yourself ...

MARGARET SILF
April 2006

There is a story growing inside you ...

Not just the proverbial one-off novel that each of us is supposed to have tucked away somewhere inside us, just waiting to be expressed. Something bigger than that.

Not even just the story of who you are, as an individual, where you come from and where you are going. Now that's a really interesting story, but it's not the whole of it. The whole story is bigger than that. Inside of you, and inside of every other one of us, there is a story gestating that is as big as the universe, and as mysterious, and as mind-blowing and as beautiful. And the amazing thing is that when we even begin to explore the narrative of this great story, we find that *we* are growing inside that story.

So, there is a story growing inside you and you are growing inside a story.

And this book is a story book in the long tradition of human story-telling. Its layers of meaning unfold in the meanings you discover for yourself. Its music lies in the resonances you detect in your own heart.

Stories have definite beginnings. They may begin 'once upon a time', but they do, definitely, begin. They have roots. They grow out of particular times and places, and they take the shape of our many and varied human cultures. Your story has a definite beginning. You probably have a birth certificate to prove it. You know when and where it begins, and you know the soil it grows out of. It's an earthed story, grounded and rooted on your particular bit of planet Earth, and nourished (or hampered) by particular people, events and encounters. It's a plant that grows in a special place, and in no other. You can't just uproot your story and plant it somewhere else where, perhaps, you *wish* it were growing, or where you maybe think it *ought* to be growing. It grows from its own roots, and in its own soil.

But where is it growing to? What is it becoming? That's another matter. That's open-ended. The outcome is still part of the great mystery. So this book is also something of a dream-book, in the best tradition of human dreaming. What do you want your story to become? What do you most desire the human story to become? And what is the dream of the great story that is guiding and nurturing your own dream?

My eye was caught by a fridge magnet in a gift shop I often frequent in the little market town of Nantwich. Fridge magnets are not where we tend to look first in our search for life wisdom, but this one, I thought, had a lot going for it. It read:

Wise parents give their children just two gifts – roots and wings.
(Holding Carter)

Not many of us who have any dealings with little children would want to quarrel with that, I thought. What more could I possibly wish to give my child than a sureness of belonging, a certain knowledge that, whatever happens, she is rooted in my love, and that this love is something she can always come home to. I want to give her sound and healthy roots that nourish her and hold her firm in the soil where she can grow.

But I need to give her wings as well. However painful it might be to watch her fly, when the time is right, her flight is the other half of the story. When I give her wings, I set her free. Free to live and discover, and shape her own unique story. Unless that happens, her story won't grow into its fullness, and neither will the great story of us all.

I guess that, however we might envisage the source of our being, we might safely assume that this foundational well of life, whom many would call 'God', would likewise give us both roots and wings – roots to nourish and sustain, and wings that set us free to fly into all our tomorrows.

The pages that follow invite you to explore your own deep roots, within the context of the story of all creation, and to risk the flight on the wings of your deepest, highest dreams. They invite you to embrace both your roots and your wings, to revere both and to be afraid of neither.

Enjoy the flight!

ANCIENT BEGINNINGS

'Creation is an ongoing process, a continual becoming.'
Robert Fripp, *Let There Be Life*

A wise creation

Everyone wants to know about their roots. Whole industries have grown up around this deep-seated human need to know where we come from. Usually a dig around the family tree, going back perhaps a few generations, satisfies our curiosity. But actually, the roots go down much, much deeper than that. So we begin our delving by stretching our horizons and our imaginations just about as far as it gets – back to the beginning of time itself. This is a Big Story, but don't let the billions and millions put you off. The purpose of the exploration is to discover – or rediscover – a sense of wonder at the sheer miracle of our being.

I have a photo that I cherish of our daughter taken when she was a small baby in her pram, gazing at a fuchsia blossom, as if the entire cosmos existed solely to bring forth this flower for her delight. That's the kind of wonder that awaits us too, if we enter into the story of life with the open eyes, hearts and minds of the very young.

As we journey, we can hardly fail to become aware of a deep wisdom pervading all that exists. You can discover the traces of this wisdom wherever you look.

Go to Alaska, and see how the bald eagle 'knows' exactly when to mate so that the chicks arrive at the same time as the homecoming salmon; see how the salmon, who have spent four years in the vast Pacific Ocean, 'know' how to find their native river, and swim back to the exact location of their birth to mate, and die; see how the grizzly bear 'knows' exactly when and where the salmon will be found. A circle of life, a web of inter-dependence.

Watch an ultrasound scan of an unborn child, and marvel at how each cell 'knows' what its purpose is, as tiny limbs and organs take shape, each new cell taking up its unique role in the making of this living miracle. This is the wonder of the self-organising principle upon which life depends, and another manifestation of the wisdom that undergirds and permeates creation.

Stand beneath a starlit sky and soar outwards on the wings of science and imagination to the dawn of time, the gathering of galaxies and the pouring out of the Milky Way. Stand at balance between the forces of gravity holding everything together and the centrifugal forces thrusting everything apart. What deep wisdom balances these opposites?

Is it all down to chance?

Where do we human beings figure in such a vast cosmic story?

Are we here by accident or by design?

Is the deep wisdom of creation interested in *us*?

Who, or what, is the mystery within and around it all, and by what name shall we know it?

Will life prevail, whatever catastrophes befall, or are we on a trajectory towards inevitable extinction?

Are we the end of the line, or is there more ... ?

If these questions resonate with you, then the journey we are about to make might offer you an opportunity to explore them, without fear, and, if you feel able to do so, to share your thoughts and feelings with other spiritual explorers.

The world in a grain of sand

It was New Year's Day and we had a friend staying with us. After the excesses of the Christmas period, we were in danger of dropping into a vacuum of lethargy, and the cold, grey weather wasn't helping. So we went into hibernation mode for the morning, lit a fire, snuggled into easy chairs and switched on the television to watch the New Year concert from Vienna. I had inwardly decided it would be a day for vegetating. In fact it has become one of my most memorable mornings, because I was to find myself dancing to the music of the spheres almost before I realised where I was!

Is that an exaggeration? Judge for yourself ...

The transmission from Vienna began in a fairly conventional way. We watched the orchestra tuning up, and the audience taking their seats in an atmosphere of excited anticipation. The music started. The familiar Viennese waltzes resounded round the concert hall and our own living room, but what really brought the whole thing to life for me was the way the film crew and presenters interspersed coverage of the concert itself, with fascinating footage of other things going on in Vienna that morning, and of the city itself.

So we were treated to scenes from Vienna life at large. We watched people of all ages, skating joyfully round the outdoor ice rink. We joined people meandering around the old city streets. We saw ballet perform- ances going on in other parts of the concert hall. We were introduced to some of the city's fine architecture, and we roamed her beautiful parks with their shy wintering wildlife. And we zoomed in with the TV cameras to observe the faces of various musicians in the orchestra and individuals in the audience, each one hinting at the secrets of a specific human life, and revealing a unique response to the music. The whole programme was a huge celebration of life.

As I watched the great cast of this performance, I found myself reflect- ing on how each one of them had, only a few short years before, been just a single cell. From that single cell had developed, over time, a person with the most amazing body, capable of growing, sustaining, renewing and reproducing itself, as well as skating, singing and dancing and a million other possibilities. From each cell had evolved a mind potentially capable of shaping cathedrals, composing symphonies, planting parks and designing televisions. From each cell had emerged a spirit fired with imagination and creativity, the desire and the ability to share its celebrations and its sorrows, and the amazing capacity to reflect upon its own origins and destiny. Life, indeed, had become conscious of itself and the wonder of its being, and each one of us was part of it.

And the backdrop to the 'performance' was no less awesome. I thought back over the vast sweep of the story of life on this earth from four billion years ago, when the first living cells appeared, through to the astounding complexity of who we are today, and I found myself wondering about all that we still have the potential to become. I thought of how a primeval bacterium, infinitesimally small, had evolved into a being who could respond consciously to the wonder of life, and turn that wonder into notes of music, vibrations upon the string of a violin, intricate movements of an ice dance, and the love of another person, and of the world.

And then my imagination took me even further back to the roots of my own being, and the roots of all human life. I reflected on how, according to present thinking in the world of astrophysics, the universe of which we are aware began around fifteen billion years ago as a single microcosmic 'seed', a pack of concentrated energy much smaller than a grain of salt, but containing the power to fling billions of galaxies into space and initiate the unfolding of everything we know, and ever shall know, of life.

I gazed at the orchestra and audience in the Vienna Concert Hall, and across the room at my friend. Just single cells who, in a few short years have become players and movers in this dance of life, capable both of pondering and responding to this Mystery.

You too are a player and a mover in this great cosmic dance, along with the stars and the ants, the astronauts and the violinists, the skaters and the shoppers. What is your own unique note in this symphony of life? How would you express it to yourself?

Take a moment to reflect on how you too have grown from a single cell, and of all the potential that came delivered in that cell. How do you feel about how that potential is unfolding?

Spend a little time amid the thrust of everyday life somewhere – maybe in a market place or a busy shopping centre, at a concert or at a fairground or in a park – anywhere where there is life! Just notice all that is going on around you, and ponder how all these activities, all these expressions of what it means to be alive, have emerged out of millions of years of evolution.

Does this look like blind chance to you? Or does it bear the marks of a creating wisdom, drawing meaning out of chaos, life out of non-being? What do you really feel?

That morning something wanted to burst inside me like its own 'big bang', and explode with the wonder of it all. It was an experience of deep-down, heartfelt *awe* at the vitality and vibrancy of it all. It made me want to take off my shoes and acknowledge that the ground I stand on – this whole planet Earth, and the universe in which it moves and lives, is holy ground.

Suppose that all of us, whatever our background or beliefs, could discover anew real and shared reasons to stand in awe before the holiness of life? The universe story gives us good reason to do so, and the energy that brought forth the universe we inhabit is the same energy that makes us desire to respond to it.

In the beginning was a seed, the size of a grain of salt.
The seed was packed with potential.

The seed held the power to bring forth, to create,
It held the power of life itself.

And the seed released its power in a big bang,
Giving birth to time and space,

And the power flowed forth, and flows still, fifteen billion years later.
And the power was, is and always will be about life.

The seed contained everything that would bring forth
Life in all its fullness.

And the secrets of the seed revealed themselves,
Through the silent reaches of the unfolding aeons,

Seeding the stars and the galaxies,
Shaping and sifting, gathering and dispersing,

Energising space with the forces that both hold us together and urge us to grow,
Each in the direction of our true nature,

Bringing forth elementary particles,
Holding all in perfect balance,

Forming primeval relationships,
Between particles and anti-particles, protons and neutrons

Surfing the knife-edge of possibility,
Creating everything out of nothing.

What inspires you to 'stand in awe'?
What takes your breath away and makes your heart feel like bursting?
Try writing, or painting, or singing or dancing your own heart's deep response to
life, or simply share your feelings with a trusted friend.

Made of stardust?

I first came across this phrase during a visit to the observatory in the grounds of our local university. The phrase hit me in the eye, in the form of a large poster above the desk of one of the astrophysicists who worked there. It proclaimed: 'We are made of stardust.'

Is it a fact, or just a rather beautiful analogy?

Let's take up the cosmic story. Some five billion years after the originating 'seedburst', a star died. It was a second-generation star, rich in the elements that we know and can name today: carbon, nitrogen, oxygen, molybdenum, calcium, magnesium, tungsten, copper, vanadium, phosphorus, sulphur, osmium, gallium, rhodium, silver, titanium, palladium, germanium, cadmium and many more. But this star was destined for a spectacular end, the explosive brilliance of a supernova – extreme violence and extreme beauty, releasing its abundance of elements into the ever-expanding realms of intergalactic space.

The death of this star and others like it was the beginning of something abundantly new. The elements released in this moment of cosmic convulsion are the elements that now shape our physical bodies.

So, not just a vivid image, but a fact: the elements that make up your body were generated in a star and were released into Life ten billion years ago by that star's supernova death.

But, a beautiful analogy too, because it tells us something deeply true: death and destruction can be the gateway to unimaginable new life. Jesus of Nazareth tells us the same truth in different words:

'Unless a seed falls into the ground and dies, it will not bear fruit'

and then goes on to reveal the deepest human meanings of this fact in his own living and dying, as we will discover later in our journey.

For now, let's just stay with the awesome fact that we are literally made of stardust, that the elements that make up our own bodies were present in time and space ten billion years ago, and that each cell of life carries, in some mysterious way, an imprinted memory of its ten billion year story.

We might draw a comparison with a different kind of 'seedburst' that was the precursor to our own conception. When a man and woman come together in sexual union, there is also a huge outpouring of potential, as millions of sperm are released to journey in search of a waiting ovum. Each one is like another 'grain of salt', carrying the potential to contribute to the coming-to-be of a whole new human life, with a unique configuration of gifts and characteristics, and able to become aware of, and respond to, the great sweep of life into which he or she will be born. Each sperm carries half of the potential 'personal universe' of a person who is being dreamed into being, just as a supernova explosion carries the potential of a million worlds.

At your conception, most of those sperm died, but one found its destination and triggered the beginning of *you*. In each one of us, at our conception, lies a potential universe of possibility.

Your life is rooted in cosmic events that happened billions of years ago. You are made of the elements that were present in the supernova death of a star. Through you flows the stream of creative, restless energy that pulses through space and time.

Take a moment simply to be present to these realities and notice, and perhaps share, your feelings.

Don't be afraid to contemplate these vast timescales. If God is the source of the Wisdom that brings all this into being and sustains and grows it all, why would a vast God be any the less credible than the smaller versions we have tried to domesticate in our religious formulations?

If you could express your feelings to the creating power shaping and energising all the stars in the universe, what might you want to say? Many people, of different faith traditions or of none, would call this creating power 'God'. What name do you give to the life-generating and life-sustaining power and wisdom from whom you spring? What does it mean to you?

Dark matter

I live near a small market town in the midlands of England. If you were to walk around it by day you would think it was quintessentially English, with its market stalls and flower beds, its small shops and neat gardens, its clock tower and guild hall. I never thought of it as anything other than this, until I had reason to collect a teenage daughter occasionally on a Friday or Saturday night, after she had spent an evening with her friends in this inoffensive town. Then it was a very different story.

The obscure little alleyways between the shops, that you would hardly notice by day, were actually entrances to clubs and bars that came alive at night, seething with youngsters beneath the glare of neon lights you never knew were there. The shops and gardens faded into the shadows, and the town took on a completely different, and almost sinister character. The Jekyll and Hyde effect of it all shocked me considerably the first time I encountered it, not least because the experience brought me face to face with the fact that here was a youth culture that felt completely alien to me. The place where I enjoyed meandering in daylight had become a place where I felt considerably threatened after dark, a place where I would not have ventured alone. I was a stranger on my own home turf.

Darkness makes a difference. And maybe you have reservations about the awesomeness and the wonder of the cosmic story. Maybe what you feel isn't awe and wonder at all, but panic and existential alone-ness when you stand beneath the stars and ponder what it's all about? Maybe your life experience has cast more shadows than sunlight, and life itself feels more like a threat than a promise? Maybe the 'sweetness and light' take on God and Life leaves you cold and has even alienated you from traditional religious practice?

It was once thought that if we could get our heads around everything in the visible universe, we would come close to understanding how it all hangs together. Particle physics put an end to that, revealing that at the underlying, sub-atomic level, the only thing that is certain is uncertainty, and nothing we can observe is reliable, because the very fact of observing it can make it change.

And as if that wasn't enough, astronomers began to observe that the visible universe wasn't working according to their predictions. In fact the only way to explain the movements of the stars and galaxies we *can* see is to assume the presence of a great deal of material that we *can't* see. This is the dark matter, and it may constitute 90 per cent of the universe, if the estimates of its gravitational pull are correct.

This is extraordinary news. It means that an enormous proportion of what we thought we understood reasonably well turns out to be completely mysterious – as yet scientists have no real idea about what 'dark matter' really is. Martin Rees (in *Our Cosmic Habitat*) points out one of the psychological effects of this: 'Particle chauvinism has to go; we're not made of the dominant stuff in the universe. We, the stars, and the visible galaxies are just traces of sediment – almost a seeming afterthought – in the cosmos; something quite different (and still unknown) controls its large-scale structure and eventual fate.'

But there is another kind of 'dark matter' that affects each of us more immediately. Which of us has never said, when reflecting on a reaction or response we have made: 'I really don't know where that came from'? So much of what we do and say, at the surface level of our existence, or think with our conscious minds, is actually just the tip of a huge, invisible ice-berg. We are shaped and affected by everything that has ever happened to us, and the influence of all those we have ever been in relationship with. Deep unconscious layers of ourselves and of each other guide and steer us in ways we cannot begin to understand.

Thinking about this can be at least as scary as contemplating the vast tracts of the unseen universe and all its mysterious potential. We tend to see the sinister side, just as I saw the sinister side of my Friday-night-after-dark home town. It appeared sinister to me because it was unknown, and what is unknown is usually felt by humankind to be threatening. In fact that nocturnal life was seething with young people, full of energy and potential, even though that energy appeared to me to be chaotic.

Perhaps the dark matter of the universe is a bit like this: fear-inspiring, because we don't know what it is or what it might be doing, but also full of energy and potential that we don't understand? Can we trust it? Do we have a choice?

In the same way, the 'dark matter' that shapes us (and all those we know and live with) so profoundly in our unconscious depths has energy and potential. How can we trust it? How can we live with it, when we don't know what it might be going to do next?

Trust, whether of God, of the cosmos, of other people or of oneself, can't be manufactured. It can only be experienced. You might like to try this little exercise:

Wherever you are, when you have a few minutes to be quietly reflective, just sit or stand still and become aware of the force of gravity holding you to the earth. Nothing can undermine this (unless you rocket yourself deliberately out of orbit). Every moment of your life you take this fact completely for granted. You never worry in the morning when you get up that today you might fly off into deep space. You don't put weights inside your shoes, just in case. Just let that awareness of the pull of gravity deepen in you for a while.

Now let this awareness turn into meditation. Very often the patterns of nature point to the patterns of the soul. This suggests a big question ...

Can you also trust that at the core of your being, the essence of your spiritual self, your true identity, you are likewise held by a force even more powerful than that of gravity – more powerful, because it is the wisdom of the universe of which gravity is only one manifestation?
Can you relate to this deep wisdom and trust that it is holding you not only 'in place', but in a unique place that only you can fill, a place of personal destiny?

In the cosmos, the dark matter exerts a gravitational pull that scientists can measure. It is a large part of what makes the cosmos hold together. Can you trust that the 'dark matter' that shapes your unconscious self is also an essential, though mysterious, part of who you are and who you are becoming?

You can't force this kind of deep trust in the mystery of things, but you can allow yourself to be open to its possibilities, and perhaps share your feelings with a trusted friend.

A dream takes shape

Over the years I seem to have gathered a number of treasures – often objects that people have given me, that have taken on particular meanings for me. Let me introduce you to two of them.

The first is a musical instrument from East Africa. It is ageless – simply a dried jacaranda seedpod, half a metre long, with its seeds still inside it. When shaken, it produces a rhythm that can carry you away to the scenes of ancient tribal dances. Such instruments have been used for millennia, and have never lost their power to entrance.

The second is an Ethiopian cross. It was given to me by a group of pilgrims with whom I shared a retreat weekend. They told me the story of a little girl from Ethiopia, who had been adopted by a couple in their community many years ago, when she was an orphaned toddler in Addis Ababa. The child had grown and flourished among them, and her presence had made them acutely aware of the great need in her home-land. And so a special relationship has sprung up between their two communities.

Why these two treasures in particular? Well, they have their roots in two special places: Tanzania and Ethiopia. These two lands lie, like two sentinels, a Gog and a Magog, to the south and the north of the Equator respectively, in East Africa. They are (to me at least) lands shrouded in mystery – ancient lands, whose stories stretch way beyond the reach of the hand of history and whose soil was to become the cradle of human life. Their equatorial location resonates with their central role in our story – the Big Story.

Let's listen in to an early instalment of that story now. Listen with the ears of imagination, knowing that what you are hearing is also the voice of history – the kind of history you read not in books but in fossils.

The place is Laetoli in Tanzania; the time, three and half million years ago. There has recently been a volcanic eruption, and the land is covered in volcanic ash. Flash floods have turned this ash into a sea of mud. Two, or three, (opinions vary) hominid creatures, possibly two adults and a child, make their way through this mud field, and leave their footprints behind, as they seek to escape from the devastation.

These footprints were – by happy (for us!) chance – buried under further volcanic ashfall, and thus became fossilised, to be discovered in

1978 by a team led by Mary Leakey, when they would amaze the palaeontologists with their revelation. Known as the Laetoli Footprints, they tell us that early hominids were bipedal as long as three and a half million years ago. The journey towards 'becoming human' was definitely underway!

Why would this early history of hominid development have anything to do with our spiritual journey? Well, walking upright had certain effects, one at least of which has honourable mention in the book of Genesis. The creature that walks upright needs to modify its skeleton. Walking on four legs functions well enough when the internal organs are safely housed within the ribcage. Not so, when we raise ourselves to bipedalism. At this stage in the journey towards 'becoming human', the pelvis becomes narrower and more like a bowl so that it can support the internal organs to make bipedal walking possible. A side effect of this is that bipedal creatures experience much more pain in giving birth than their four-legged forebears.

An intuition that this reflects something of the earliest chapters of our 'becoming human' comes across in the archetypal story recounted in the book of Genesis:

> To the woman God said:
> 'I will multiply your pains in childbearing,
> you shall give birth to your children in pain.' (Genesis 3:16)

Traditionally, we understand this matter of pain in childbearing as some kind of punishment for wrongdoing in Eden – but what if it were actually a sign of our progression, from an earlier to a more advanced stage of physical evolution?

Punishment or progress? Maybe we can hold on to that question, because it will come up again ...

Walking upright brought other possibilities in its wake. It enabled us to keep a better lookout for possible danger in the savannah, and to spot the lions before they spotted us. It freed us to use our 'front legs' for other things, like carrying tools, and children, and using our new-found hands to shape the world around us. And it was the preamble (if you'll excuse the pun!) to our next great leap forward – the Bigger Brain, as we shall soon discover.

So, those footprints in the volcanic ash may have been just a small step for three creatures fleeing from a volcano, but they were a huge leap towards humankind. And the Genesis writers seem to have had a hunch about this, as they try to describe the wonder of our 'becoming' in the creation story.

Even so, 'the ape who walks upright' is still a long way from human – still very much simply a physical entity, part of the food chain, living from hand to mouth under the ruthless law of 'eat or be eaten'. Yet those footprints point the way ahead, to a being with its roots in these early stages of evolution, but its wings spread to fly far beyond these horizons. Those footprints point forwards towards you and me.

Before we take flight, however, we might just pause to reflect on our feelings as we ponder these ancient beginnings of our human story.

How do you feel about your own physical being – your bodily presence in this world?

Humankind evolved from creatures who were purely physical, long before we can speak of something like 'mind'. Many of us now tend to regard our bodies as an unfortunate extra that we have to carry around with us, while our minds get on with important matters and our spirits soar to higher things. This raises questions about our whole relationship with our physical self:

Do you think of your body as a friend or an enemy of your soul, an ally or a hindrance on your spiritual journey? A gift to be cherished, or a problem to be fought and overcome?

Depending on your answer, how would you now choose to treat your body? Is there anything specific that you would want to change in your present lifestyle? Do you ever feel like saying 'thank you' to your body for all it does for and with you? What kind of 'thank you' might it appreciate? (For example, regular walks, healthier food, a bit more rest, a change of air, liberation from some addictive substance, a chance to unwind at least once a week?)

But the child who learns to walk soon reaches the 'terrible twos', when he is convinced that the world should revolve around him and she is determined to have her way in all matters. The becoming-human being also has to learn that nothing has meaning, except in relationship with everything else. We are created to be 'we'. We are part of the great web of being.

The web of Life

What images does the word 'web' evoke for you?

When I think of webs, and weaving, I think of several things …

A web reminds me of the deep underground network of life that supports the trees I see around me. The bit of the tree I can see is only a small part of the whole story. Whatever is above ground depends utterly on an unseen root system that both holds it and sustains it. I'm like a tree myself. The visible 'me' is held in being, nourished and supported, by a vast root network that stretches far back, even to the beginning of time, and deep down, into my own history and the story of us all.

It also reminds me that simply to stay alive for just one more minute, I am dependent on the flow of life-blood through many miles of a complex circulatory system and the action of millions of electrical pulses through a nervous system far more sophisticated than any computer system that human minds can as yet devise.

And then, of course, there is the world wide web, the internet, that can connect us to others all over the world, in seconds, and pulses ceaselessly with our messages, like a vast system of arteries, veins and capillaries, keeping every remote part of the body of humanity connected.

Webs, whether they are a network of connections, with people and with creation, that nourish and support us, or whether they are networks of information through which our minds can communicate, remind us of our *interdependence*. No man is an island, and every single creature on earth depends for its own existence on the existence of others. The mystics of all faith and wisdom traditions have always taught us this foundational truth, and native spiritualities continue to reflect it. Now, in the twentieth and twenty-first centuries, science is telling us the same thing. Every particle in creation is interrelated with every other particle, and what happens to one part of creation affects all of creation.

This afternoon I walked to the post office to send off some letters. As I climbed the hill on my homeward journey, I got to thinking about what I had done today, and whether any of it, at all, could have been done in isolation. You might like to reflect on your own day in this light …

*What have you done today? Could you have done any of it without the help –
seen or unseen – of other people or other parts of creation? Perhaps you have*

had lunch. Did you grow the food yourself? Harvest it? Package it? Transport it? Did you make the pots and pans you cooked it in, or the fuel supply that heated it up? Did you fire the pottery you ate it from, or forge the cutlery you ate it with? Did you go to work, or to town? Did you make your own car or drive your own bus, or stitch your own shoes? Did you lay the pavements that you walked along? Did you grow the trees you saw, or hatch the wild birds that sang to you? Did you switch on the sun this morning, or blow out the moon last night? Did you fix the level of oxygen in the atmosphere, so that it sustains you without burning you up? Did you adjust gravity this morning, to make sure that you wouldn't fly off into space? Indeed, did you bring yourself to birth, bring yourself up, teach yourself to talk, single-handedly turn that single cell that was your beginning into all the complex organs that keep you alive?

But enough of the silly questions! We all know that we are part of an interrelated and totally interdependent community of life – only some-times it's good to remind ourselves, lest we fall into the dangerous delusion of self-sufficiency.

The truth is, we, and all creatures, are made for relationship. We are part of a wholeness, and what happens to any of us affects all of us. The different native spiritualities understand this a lot better than the more sophisticated religious or social systems. The Native American Chief Seathl, for example, reminds us powerfully of our interconnectedness, and the extreme danger of living out of kilter with it:

> We are part of the earth and it is part of us.
> The perfumed flowers are our sisters; the deer,
> The horse, the great eagle, these are our brothers.
> The rocky crests, the juices in the meadow, the body heat
> Of the pony and man – all belong to the same family.
> This we know. The earth does not belong to man; man belongs
> To the earth. This we know. All things are connected like
> The blood which unites one family. All things are connected.
> Whatever befalls the earth befalls the sons of the earth.
> Man did not weave the web of life; he is merely a strand in it.
> Whatever he does to the web he does to himself.
>
> (from Chief Seathl's Testament)

You might like to take this testament into a period of reflection, and perhaps share your reactions and feelings about it with a friend.

Stories within stories

It's not often that there is time for calm reflection first thing in the morning: either I'm in a daze or in a rush, and there is usually nothing in between these two extremes. But on one particular morning I woke to the inpouring of dawn light through my bedroom window, and had the luxury of time simply to come round gently, and absorb the living presence of all that surrounded me. It is an experience that has never left me.

As I lay in bed I looked up at the ceiling, which is clad in pirana pine – a beautiful softwood with delicate graining and streaks of variegated colour. And around me stood the pine furniture. Not so long ago all this wood was growing in the forests of the world. My mind travelled back to forests I had known and loved, especially the rain forests of Eastern Australia, or the ancient stands of Cathedral Grove on Vancouver Island, or the dark swathes of pine covering acres of Eastern Europe, or quite simply the woods at the bottom of the garden of my childhood home in Yorkshire.

Fifty years ago I played in these woods. Just a couple of years ago I wandered amid the canopy of the Queensland forests, watching the pademelons hopping around in the early light. But actually these forests have a story which began with the emergence of the first wood cell 370 million years ago. My ceiling, my bed, my desk, my cupboards and shelves are one with them. Every molecule in them was present in the primeval rain forests. I want to thank the wood around me in the room for being there. I want to thank the source of all being for shaping these molecules so lovingly into forest and furniture. Somehow it makes my bedroom feel like a sacred grove, and I become acutely aware of how much I owe creation for its gifts to me.

Then I feel the cotton of the duvet cover and sheet, and remember the cotton fields where it grew, and the hands that picked it, and turned it into sheets and pillowcases. I remember the sun and rain caressing the cotton fields, and the earth that held the roots and nourished them. I reflect on how my pillowslip was made of earth and light and water, that themselves were present in aeons beyond my imagination – billions of years in the making. Every fibre of my duvet cover remembers this universal story. It covers me for just a few years every night – just a brief fragment of a mighty narrative!

I gaze at the picture hanging on the wall beside my bed – the one our daughter gave us the first Christmas after she had left home to go to university. I think of the paper, and how it too has grown in primeval forests. I think of the pigments, and remember how ancient native peoples first extracted them from the clay of the earth. I think of how humankind first discovered the possibility of expressing the visions of the mind in ways that could be shared, in cave paintings and all the art forms that followed after.

All of these stages were leading to the vision expressed in this particular picture, itself made of paper and pigment, vision and experience, uniquely shaped into shareable form by this particular artist – and now becoming a gateway through which my own senses can lead me closer to my roots in God. A static picture, but a momentous and dynamic narrative. Placed into my hands by a beloved daughter at a particular and poignant moment in *our* shared narrative.

But I can't lie here all day in this state of reverie. I look at my watch – and I'm off again! It too has its own story to tell. A story of primeval convulsions that shaped this little planet, tearing mountains apart and heaving continents together, leaving trails of iron and gold in the entrails of the embryonic Earth. The metals of my watch were there among it all.

I think of humankind grappling with the concept of time – of the early engineers who first made clocks – of the body of experience they built on, the long aeons of learning to make tools, the even longer aeons when fingers were evolving that would one day hold those tools. I think of our earliest ancestors who first noticed (long before they could articulate the wonder of it) the coming of the sunlight at dawn and its departing at dusk, and how the interval between these sacred moments would vary according to the season. My watch was there when Stonehenge was shaped and when the first shaft of solstice dawnlight penetrated the gap between the stones of prehistoric burial mounds like Newgrange in Ireland and flooded the inner chambers with light.

My watch was there when Egyptian astronomers observed the stars and mirrored their shapes and movements in the pyramids. My watch came to me at a meaningful moment in my own narrative – my leaving of paid employment, in the year 2000. A very significant moment in time – not just my own milestone but the millennium milestone for all earth-dwellers. My watch is part of an ancient narrative, and now it records the passing moments of my own story, and I thank God for it.

In this ancient narrative, still unfolding in the here and now, all is one, and your story, and mine, are woven into it.

Take a while to be still in a favourite place, perhaps in your home, or elsewhere, and listen deeply to the stories embedded in everything around you. Share your reflections with a friend if you can.

Savannah legacy

I went for a walk one morning. As I set off, I noticed an old can lying in a neighbour's drive. Seeing it there made me more aware of all the other litter lying around – the detritus of our modern living that we strew so thoughtlessly upon the natural world. On my way home I picked the can up and put it in the bin for recycling. No big deal, but it set me thinking about those millions of years of life on the savannah which we inherit. It wasn't all about the wonder of life, and the joyous awareness of how we are all one in the web of life. It certainly wasn't a garden of Eden in the way we perhaps would like to imagine it. The savannah is a place of huge potential, but there is 'litter' lying there too – litter that affects the way we are today. Robert Winston puts it like this:

> *This Garden of Eden … was not a land of plenty, with fruit hanging in abundance from every tree and fattened calves meekly waiting to be slaughtered. Finite resources – of prey, edible vegetation, water and shelter – could mean that there was competition for resources. Not just competition between species, but competition within the species. In other words, we might well have been at war with one another.* (Human Instinct)

Life on the savannah was red in tooth and claw, as each creature struggled for survival, and the relentless hierarchy of the food chain asserted itself. If you have ever watched wild life programmes on television, and shuddered to see a lion or leopard bringing down a zebra or an antelope, you will not be tempted to romanticise these, our ancient beginnings. It would be nice to think that we are well beyond all that, but sadly it isn't so. The instinct for survival, if necessary at the expense of other creatures, including our own species, is still going strong. We continue to experience the same paralysing fears that our early ancestors did – fears that still prepare our bodies for 'fight or flight' whether we will or no. In Winston's words, *'while living in a very advanced modern world, we all do so with Stone Age brains and bodies.'*

This raises another big question:

Many people raised within a traditional religious system have been taught about a perfect paradisal state which we once inhabited, and from which we were expelled because we committed an 'original sin'. How do you feel about this kind

of teaching? How does it resonate with your experience of being part of an
unfolding story of life?

Don't be too hasty in reaching a conclusion, and don't throw the baby
out with the bath water. As we explore further, you may discover that
there is deeper truth in these stories than meets the eye, but to discover
it, we need to be honest with ourselves and each other about the facts and
feelings of our ancient story. For now, just notice your reactions to this
apparent clash between religious teaching and the evidence of science,
and share them, if you wish, with one or more soul-friends.

In fact we all inherit the instinctual drives of the earliest hominids and
indeed of their forebears. When it comes to survival we will feel the fear
of the open plains whenever we sense that we are under threat. We may
respond with violence rather than tenderness to the urging of an overwhelming desire to pass on our genes in a sexual act. We go on engaging
in the relentless struggle for scarce resources, motivated primarily by
'what's best for me'. This has always been the price of physical survival so
far, and we are still bound into that price.

At the physical level we are still very much at the mercy of our
instincts. Are these instinctual drives the result of some kind of 'fall from
grace' in some imagined perfect state from which we were banished,
battle-scarred and condemned to death? Or are they our natural
inheritance, from the purely physical world from which our bodies have
evolved?

A further question presents itself, however. Do we have any choice
about how we react? Do we have to remain merely at the bidding of our
instincts?

I picked up the offending can and recycled it. Perhaps I can do something like that with some of my wilder instincts. Perhaps, for example, the
survival instinct that can turn me into a fighter if provoked can be
recycled into the kind of energy that pours itself into a different kind of
fight – a fight for justice in an unjust world, on behalf of those whose
voices are suppressed. Perhaps my instinctual fears can be recycled into a
deeper empathy with others who may have more reason to live in fear
than I do. Perhaps my instinct to hoard resources for my own use can be
recycled into a recognition that there is more joy in sharing than in
hoarding.

Which of these two statements resonates more powerfully with your own
feelings about life?

'I am a fallen sinner and humankind as a whole is a lost cause, because we are condemned to death as a consequence of original sin'

or

'I carry, in every cell of my body, the instinctual legacy of the savannah, but I, and all humankind, have now evolved to a stage where we can use our minds to make choices about how we control these instincts and use them for the common good.'

Wipeout?

It's not just the predators that threaten life on the savannah, or, indeed, life on planet earth in any stage of its 'becoming'. The Big Story is also littered with the debris of catastrophes and extinctions.

These come in a variety of guises. Take a deep breath now, because the ride is getting rough.

Great Ice Ages froze planet Earth over two billion years ago, and soon afterwards the oxygen crisis struck. Unprecedented levels of oxygen were released into the earth's atmosphere, causing massive disruption in the biosphere, and a catastrophic scale of destruction for almost all of the primitive life forms on earth at the time. Life dealt with this disaster by mutating into forms that could deal with oxygen, and the art of breathing was under way. This near-extinction had been transformed into new and more creative ways of being alive, with the beginning of respiration.

The second era of life on earth also came to a very chilly end 570 million years ago, when the planet was almost totally glaciated and 80 to 90 per cent of all species were eliminated. In the words of Brian Swimme and Thomas Berry:

> An entire era with two billion years of adventure came to its shuddering close, but its biological inventions would weather even this vast glacial extinction and rebound to establish a new episode in Earth's adventure.
>
> (The Universe Story)

If we move on to 245 million years ago, we come upon news that would not sound out of place on our twenty-first century television screens: climate change! Whatever the reason – and scientists remain unsure – massive climate destabilisation destroyed something between 75 and 90 per cent of all the species then populating the Earth. Millions of years of the natural building up of an interrelated life community was destroyed. The few survivors were compelled to discover new ways of relating to each other and moving the adventure of life forwards. That we exist today is a testimony to their success.

A further mass extinction swept the face of the earth 67 million years ago, and is well documented in the science notebooks of most primary school children, because it famously eliminated the dinosaurs. But once again it was a cloud with a silver lining, because the removal from earth of so much competition made way for a rapid explosion of many different life forms, including, most significantly for us, the placental mammals.

Some eight million years ago another huge ecological disaster caused further mass extinctions, and destroyed the forests that then covered large tracts of the planet, leaving extensive grasslands in their wake. This marked the end of the reign of the apes on planet earth, and the beginning of a very different kind of creature, the bipedal hominid – our earliest hominoid ancestors. The resulting savannah was to become the cradle of human life as we know it today.

So the concept of endangered species or global climate change is nothing new to earth's story, except that now one species, our own, has the power to bring about such catastrophe single-handedly and consciously. However, there are important patterns we might observe in this long litany of destruction.

First, a new surge of creativity invariably emerges out of a period of instability, and life unfolds in greater diversity than before whenever it takes a shock wave in its stride.

The Genesis story of Noah, which is paralleled in most of the creation myths of humankind, is a beautifully poetic way of expressing the intuition that the radically new always springs from a situation that feels like chaos, and dark desolation, but that a creating, life-generating spirit is at work in these situations. The interplay of the presence of chaos and the ordering dynamic of creation are constant and intimate partners in the unfolding story of life.

So where does this leave us in our exploration of our deep roots in the Big Story? What about our own situations? When I reflect on my own life I see a frequently recurring pattern of events that seemed close to catastrophic at the time. Admittedly, my own mini-dramas don't rate any mention on the world stage, but for me, if for no one else, they were all-consuming when I was embroiled in them. However, in hindsight, I see that nearly always something new grew out of those times of turmoil. There was often a breakthrough in the heart of the breakdown. I would go so far as to say that pretty well everything I have learned in life that was worth learning has been learned in the ruins of previous hopes and expectations. For this reason I feel rather sorry for people who live smooth and unproblematic lives, if, indeed, there *are* any such people.

What does your story reveal in the way of disasters, and has there been any blessing in the curse? When do you feel your personal growth has accelerated? What was the cause of the shift?

At a global level, this pattern is graphically demonstrated in the Christian story of the crucifixion and resurrection of Jesus of Nazareth, in whom, Christians believe, all human breakdown was transmuted into break-through on an eternal scale.

A second pattern that earth's story reveals makes it clear that though new life forms and new levels of complexity and adaptability emerge from the recurring times of chaos, there is no guarantee of survival for any particular species. At the level of the particular, there is often a sacrifice, yet at the level of the universal thrust of life, there is always progress. Paul Davies (*God and the New Physics*) speaks of this phenome-non in terms of 'closed' and 'open' systems. A particular species is a closed system with its own ways of doing things, and as such it is subject to the laws of entropy and the risk of extinction. Life itself, however, is an open system, a total and holistic system, and will always emerge victorious, to continue to evolve to new levels. It is, in this sense, 'eternal'.

This raises difficult questions for the human species which has traditionally viewed itself as the pinnacle of creation and has been very unwilling to look upon the possibility of its own demise.

Do you think creation has 'peaked' in homo sapiens, or are we going further? If so, in what direction? Can you contemplate the idea that homo sapiens might face extinction? Where would life go next?

Where next?

Three sets of footprints in the volcanic ash … where are they leading? Is the human family on planet Earth going anywhere, or are we just another species that will 'blossom and perish as leaves on a tree'? Such questions have preoccupied humankind for as long as we have been thinking, questing people.

As we leap the threshold into the next stage of our questing, there is another big question to ponder …

What do we think this quest is actually about?

Perhaps I can offer you two different approaches, and invite you to reflect on which of them, if either (or both), resonates with your own intuitions and feelings …

Is the prime purpose of our human spiritual quest to discover the answers to our deep-seated questions about the meaning of life and to formulate them into a scientific 'theory of everything' or a definitive and unquestionable creed?

Or is our human quest focused primarily on the call and the challenge to become, and to keep on becoming, ever more fully human?

Are we more concerned to explain, or to explore?

How do you feel?

If we think for a moment about where these two different approaches to our quest would lead us, we might notice very different consequences.

If our main aim and purpose is to 'find the answer' and 'solve the problem' for once and for all, then it is likely that every individual, every culture and every faith tradition would come up with a different result. This would lead to competition, and the attitude of 'my answer is the right one, therefore all others must be wrong'. Sounds familiar?

If, however, our primary aim and purpose is to continue to evolve ever more fully into what it means to be fully, 100 per cent human, then there need be no such competition. We would surely realise that each individual, each culture, each branch of human knowledge and each faith tradition would have unique insights to bring to this quest. Sounds attractive?

So far in our journey together we have been exploring the early chapters in the story of life on this planet, and how, over aeons of time, there has been movement closer and closer to *homo sapiens*, the rational being. Life itself, at least on this planet, and from our point of view appears to have an agenda of bringing forth what is more and more human.

As this story unfolds further, we will, I believe, discover ever-new layers of the emergence of our full humanity. If on the way we discover 'answers', those answers will probably only raise more and more new questions to grow and stretch us further towards the fullness of our humanity.

The ramifications of this evolving journey may challenge us to the core, yet I suggest that it is the most thrilling enterprise we could imagine, and one in which each one of us is invited to be fully and consciously engaged.

So where *do* the footprints of our distant forebears lead us next ... ?

A CONTRACT WITH LIFE

*'L'hominisation est sans doute inachevée et l'humani-
sation encore bien fragile.'*

*('Hominisation is undoubtedly not yet complete,
and humanisation is still pretty fragile.')*

(Sign in the Evolution section of the Cité des Sciences
museum, Paris)

Enter the bigger brain

Let's fast forward now, to approximately 150,000 years ago, carrying, as we go, the second of my 'treasures' from Africa – the Ethiopian cross.

In Kibish, in Ethiopia, a man dies. Not a world-shattering event, but his skull would be discovered by a Kenyan fossil hunter in 1967. This discovery is currently thought to be an example of the first modern human – *homo sapiens*.

The quest to Become Human has moved on hugely. And the main feature that might strike us is the size of the brain. Around this time in our evolution, our brains were growing, and by the advent of Neanderthal Man, brains had reached three times the size of those of the early hominids.

What is really interesting about this increase in brain size is the *reason* for it. What factors might have caused such a thing to happen? What could have triggered this big new step forward in our evolutionary story? Anthropologists suggest some fascinating possibilities.

The first is *hardship*. Around this time the Earth was in a big freeze. Most of the water was locked up in vast ice caps, and drought ruled. To survive you had to be inventive. You had to 'think outside the box', to work out fresh ways of overcoming difficulties. You even had to think ahead, in ways that would have been impossible before. The brightest and most creative won the day, and got the chance to pass on their genes. It didn't take all that long for this stream of natural selection to produce a bigger (and, even more importantly, a more *adaptive*) brain, that would become a prime characteristic of our species.

The second reason is even more interesting. It's about *relationship*. At this point in our story we were living mainly in small groups of hunter-gatherers. Life wasn't easy, and often depended on hunting down very large beasts, such as bison. Single-handedly felling a bison or a woolly mammoth wasn't an option. It called for teamwork. And so the beginnings of genuine community began to emerge. In small groups, it became obvious that what happened to any one of the group affected all of them. Interpersonal relationship became the biggest challenge, and the fossil records reveal that the parts of the brain that deal with social interaction were the parts that were growing most obviously.

Relationship – then as now – was humanity's biggest headache but also the gateway to humanity's future.

From this stage of our evolution, anthropologists speak specifically of a 'theory of mind'. The human story has moved beyond being 'just body' to being 'body plus mind'. We are no longer simply physical, and a part of the food chain. We are physical *and* rational, capable of making choices, and using our brains to work out strategies of survival.

But the power of mind is a two-edged sword. How would we use such power?

There would be good and life-giving results. We would learn almost to read each other's minds, interpreting body language to develop deep *empathy* with each other, bearing in mind that language as we now know it was not yet a feature of life. Such telepathic skills are still evident in some aboriginal peoples. We would also learn the need for a sense of *co-responsibility*. An injured companion must be cared for, since the well-being of the whole group depended on the well-being of each member. Again, the fossil evidence reveals that injured people were indeed cared for in some ways, since they can be seen to have survived for some period of time following major injury, and this would only have been possible if others had been caring for them. In due course, we learned to use our skills to develop complex language, and to pass on vital information to each other and to the next generation.

But it doesn't take too much imagination to realise that we would also have learned to use our mental powers not in the service of the group, but in the service of self at the *expense* of the group. Just as most types of animal are not backward in seizing a physical advantage over each other, it should not surprise us that we rational human beings would likewise be tempted to use our abilities to gain an advantage over one another, to deceive one another and even to do violence to each other to get our own way.

Bigger brains make all these things possible. In fact they expand the scope for self-focused behaviour enormously, and open up vast new possibilities for doing harm as well as good. And spoken language can deceive in ways that are not possible when communication is carried on mainly through body language. Lips may lie, but eyes do not.

When I reflect on how the emergence of mind could so easily, and so inevitably, have become both a blessing and a bane – something with the potential to develop in two opposing directions – one very life-giving and centred on the good of the whole community, the other potentially very destructive, and centred on personal gain, I am vividly reminded of Genesis again:

Yahweh God planted a garden in Eden, which is in the east, and there he put the man he had fashioned. From the soil, Yahweh God caused to grow every kind of tree, enticing to look at and good to eat, with the tree of life in the middle of the garden, and the tree of the knowledge of good and evil.
(Genesis 2:8-9)

The *tree of the knowledge of good and evil* ... the tree which, according to the Genesis writer, was forbidden, and which we tasted at our eternal peril. Does the advent of mind bring with it such a double-edged blade? The possibility of becoming more and more fully human, and at the same time the possibility of using our human intellect to reduce ourselves and each other to something less than human?

But this is not just 'the tree of good and evil' – not just the potential for good and ill in all we do and all we are – it is the tree of the *knowledge* of good and evil. So far, the evolution of life on this planet had been in a real sense 'unknowing'. With the advent of mind, all this changes. The human species enters into a new realm of self-conscious awareness. This brings with it the possibility of sheer wonder at the awesomeness of creation that we explored in the last section. But it also brings the knowledge that we can, in any and every situation, choose what leads to life or what brings harm. The power of reason brings with it two great gifts: the *freedom* to choose, and the *responsibility* to choose well. We may seize the freedom with both hands, but the responsibility may fill us with apprehension. In the words of the Benedictine poet Ralph Wright:

> *I fear the fact that I am made to choose*
> *And so may lose.*

The promise of progress towards the fullness of our humanity also carries with it the possibility of the diminishment or loss of that humanity, *through our own choosing.*

The challenge of choice has been with us ever since, as we shall explore shortly.

Size isn't everything

But, before we enter this new terrain of choice, there is something even more interesting to notice about how our brain, and thus our minds, evolved. It isn't just about size. It's about what goes on inside, and what we *do* with what lives between our ears. The brain has its own story, which goes back a lot further than the human story, and yet shapes our story in very powerful ways. Let's just listen to some of the echoes from that ancient story ...

The neuroscientists tell us that our human brain has various different elements, which evolved sequentially, each new addition building on and incorporating all that had gone before. Ancient parts of our brain have been around for hundreds of millions of years, while the most recent evolutionary accretion, the cortex, appeared in its present form relatively recently – marking the point from which we begin to describe ourselves as 'modern *homo sapiens*'.

Nature, it seems, always builds on what is already there, and continually seeks to bring forth an improved model, better adapted to its current circumstances. And so it is with brains.

The brain story appears to begin with something very basic and instinctual that helped early life forms, such as the reptiles keep ahead of their predators, and become better predators themselves. The ancient parts of the brain we have inherited deal with the means of survival – a pretty important function! – including skills of deception and defence, and the primitive ability to distinguish between something you can eat and something that will eat you.

Human beings no longer live from hand to mouth like this, but these ancient survival instincts and behaviour patterns still come into their own. We see them powerfully at work in the worlds of business and politics. It's not so comfortable to notice them in our interpersonal relationships. The ability to deceive, to cover our tracks, even to change our appearance, demeanour and tone of voice to suit the situation, are part of the legacy from long ago. They constitute our survival kit, and they come on line whenever we feel threatened.

As life evolved, and the early mammals appeared on the scene, a new chapter of the brain story was evolving, and has also passed its legacy down to us. This part of the unfolding miracle of thought had more to do with the nurturing skills needed by the early mammals, who now were required not only to hunt and avoid danger, but also actively to care for their offspring until the babies became capable of independent life. Relationship and emotion were now entering the field of 'mind', and the sensory perceptions were widening far beyond those available to the ancient reptiles. Mammals carry their unborn young within their own bodies, and nourish them with their own milk. From the moment of its conception every mammal is, by its very nature, in *relationship*, first with its mother, and then with the wider world. The mammalian brain has evolved to reflect and respond to the demands of relationship.

This was a big step forward, and another layer in the foundation for what would become the human mind. So far so good, but the fossil records of the early hominids suggest that for a very long time there was no apparent further development in terms of, for example, the tools we used, or the way we expressed ourselves. Some kind of limitation seems to have been present, so that our ancient ancestors simply didn't appear to question the ways they did things, or to ask 'What if we tried hunting *this* way?' or 'What would happen if we modified our flint blades like *this?*' In other words, there was no real evidence of creativity or the use of the imagination ...

... until evolution brought out the next model, incorporating the *cortex,* or higher brain.

This new level of brain made a very significant difference. It brought a sense of the *future* with it. It carried the gift of imagination. Imagination is perhaps God's best ever gift. Imagination is what enables us to bring to mind infinite possibilities about what it means to be a human being on planet Earth, and to turn those possibilities into reality. Perhaps creation itself is an outpouring of the divine imagination, and our own creativity is an expression and a manifestation of this outpouring. Yet, everything has its shadow, and the dawn of a sense of the future also brought with it the potential for anxiety about that unknown quantity.

The development of the human family took a major leap forward when the higher brain arrived. But nature never rests, and there is always a better model on the drawing board. Around 40,000 years ago the latest chapter (so far) began, as our brains evolved the potential for language and the ability to reflect in a coordinated way using all the existing aspects of the brain, including the ability to recognise when the ancient defence mechanisms are appropriate and when they are not.

And let us not forget that, so the neuro-scientists tell us, we are currently using around only 5 or 6 per cent of the full potential of our brain capacity. Most of that miraculous organ of thought and reflection that lodges in our skulls is unused! We can't even begin to imagine what it might become when it grows up – or rather, when *we* grow up!

The development of each one of us also follows the evolutionary story of all of us. We begin as a single-cell organism, and grow *in utero* and in infancy through all the stages of evolving life on Earth, all the while striving to become the person we are, just as the whole human family strives to become all it is destined to become.

Your story is indeed part of the Big Story, and it reflects it chapter by chapter.

What does the word 'imagination' mean to you?
How do you feel about the possibility that the use of imagination – the ability to think in endless possibilities and to make those possibilities into actualities – may be a crucial key to everything that still lies beyond homo sapiens?

The challenge of choice

In today's society, with all its expectations and decisions, we demand a great deal from our brains. It takes us up to twenty years or more to educate our young sufficiently for them to use their intellect to fulfil their own potential and be fruitful in society.

But what if we turn that question round, and instead of asking what we are demanding of our brains, ask instead what is our brain demanding of *us*?

The evolution of such a sophisticated organ of thought, capable of leading us from being just part of the food chain, operating on instinctual drives alone, to being reflective beings capable of pondering the ultimate mysteries and meanings of life itself, asks something in return. Circumstances confront us continually with choice. And those choices can be boiled down to some simple patterns:

- In this situation, do I choose a course of action that favours and enhances life for all creation, or will I choose to take my own advantage from the situation, regardless of the effects on others?
- Which course of action (or which response or reaction) is likely to lead to a greater humanisation of myself and of all of us? Which choices are tending to *de*humanise myself or all of us?
- Which choices are coming from that part of my being that longs for transcendence – to go beyond our present stage of being human to something much greater – and which choices are coming from the defensive parts of me that see the rest of creation as a threat to be - conquered? What is really driving my choices in any particular situation?

The quotation on the title page of this section sums things up very neatly:

> *Hominisation is undoubtedly not yet complete and humanisation is still pretty fragile.*

The process of hominisation is going very well – we have already explored some facets of it in the story of our physical evolution and the development of the brain that has become the processing power of our human mind. There is every reason to assume that this process is still ongoing.

But *homi*nisation is not the same thing as *huma*nisation. While homi-nisation (the development of *homo sapiens* as a physical being with the power of thought and imagination) is still in process, humanisation (the development of ourselves as fully human beings) has barely begun, and is very fragile.

Yet, it *has* begun, and we have good reason to trust in its continuance and fulfilment. But – and it's a very big 'but' – this isn't going to happen automatically. It will happen only to the extent that we *choose* for it to happen and strive to implement that fundamental choice.

In our evolution as the human species on planet Earth, we have reached the stage where we are endowed with the mental ability to reflect on our story, on our own actions and decisions, and to make choices either for the greater good, or for self-interest alone. Most of the world's spiritual traditions focus on this level of choice, and offer various kinds of guidance for making the better choices. The future of our species, and perhaps the future of all creation as we know it, may hang upon those choices, even the little moment-by-moment choices that we might dismiss as too small to take seriously.

This leads us to consider our 'contract with life'. What does such a 'contract' entail?

Contracts are about partnership. They embody a mutual agreement to achieve some goal together, with each party undertaking to make the necessary effort to realise this vision. Life continually honours its side of the contract with *us*, endowing us, in every new generation, with all we need to keep on becoming more fully human. The other side of the contract is down to each one of us.

Perhaps we see the beginnings of this contract in the wisdom of the Genesis writer, though sadly we have mainly been taught to read this narrative as a story of disobedience and punishment. Listen again to what God has to say to 'the fallen Adam':

> *Accursed be the soil because of you!*
> *Painfully you will get your food from it*
> *As long as you live.*
> *It will yield you brambles and thistles,*
> *As you eat the produce of the land.*
> *By the sweat of your face*
> *Will you earn your food …* (Genesis 3:17–19)

Certainly it sounds like punishment, as undoubtedly the writer intended it should. But what does it mean for *you*?

When I reflect on this image of God 'cursing' Adam and apparently condemning him to a life sentence of hard labour, I hear other echoes of

meaning. Just as God 'cursed' Eve with pain in childbirth and with relationship problems, so it appears Adam is going to have to work at life.
Things are not just going to drop in their laps. We have seen how the
'curse' of Eve is indeed fulfilled in the birthing pains that came as a result
of bipedalism and how the challenge of relationship in fact turned out to
be a major factor in the growth of our human brains. But we have also
seen that these features were characteristics of our evolving physiology
and changing social circles, not a punishment for disobedience. What,
then, if 'Adam's curse' were similarly a way of describing the felt effects of
being a creature endowed with mind and reason and choice? The fullness
of human life isn't simply going to happen, we might surmise from this.

It is something we are going to have to *work* at.

All living creatures have to work, to some extent, at getting their food,
but only the human creature has both the responsibility and the satisfaction of being called upon to work at what it means to be truly human.
Anyone who has brought up a child knows that the finished product
doesn't come gift-wrapped in the crib. Many long years of heartache and
joy go into the making of an adult man or woman, and even then the
'product' is far from finished. What has to go into the making of a truly
and fully human being?

We might conclude that the process of bringing humanity to birth is
going to be accompanied by both pain and hard work. We come back to
the big question that raised its head earlier:

Is this punishment, or is it progress?

Discovering our own responses to this question, and applying the challenge to ourselves in our own circumstances, is the context of our
personal 'contract with life'.

It involves two levels of choosing:

- A fundamental choice: do I desire to live primarily for myself alone, or
for the wider circle of the human family and of all creation?
- A lifetime of moment-by-moment choices, little and large, as to what
is the more life-giving thing to choose in any particular situation.

To embark upon a life of conscious awareness of the vision and the
potential that is drawing us forward is to embrace this challenge of
choice. It distinguishes us very powerfully from the rest of the animal
kingdom. It invites us to keep on reaching out towards all that still lies
beyond us. To be a rational being is to know that in everything we do or
say, there will be the potential for both good and evil, both for that which
leads to higher levels of humanity and for that which diminishes and
even destroys us. Always, and in everything, we can choose between

transcendence and regression. What we choose is what, ultimately we will become.

The story of Max and the slave girls

Max was a foreman in a factory in wartime Germany under the Third Reich. His factory employed Russian girls who had been conscripted into German industry as forced labour. Some of them were sick. All were undernourished. Max did his best to look after them, shielding them from the Nazi managers, helping them out with food and finding a quiet corner where the very sick among them could rest. His humanity set him on a dangerous collision course with the authorities but he stood his ground.

When the war was over the Russians marched on Berlin and occupied the factory. The Nazi managers tried to flee, for fear of reprisals, as the girls pointed out those who had oppressed them. Eventually the invading troops got to Max and were about to take him prisoner. The girls intervened: 'No,' they said, '*he* was good to us.'

Max had a saying that he used to offer his children and grandchildren as the fruit of his own life's wisdom:

'In every human situation,' he would urge them, 'be *human*.'

★ ★ ★

This is an example of what it can mean to honour the 'contract with life', living in such a way that as a result of our choices and responses, Life itself moves forward to a higher level of humanity and not back to the instinctual reflexes of 'me first and the devil take the hindmost'.

Have you seen this dynamic in action? What examples would you choose from your own experience to show what it means to 'choose life'?

Good branch? Bad branch?

Are we all engaged in some kind of primeval struggle at the heart of our psyche? If so, how might we get a handle on what is going on?

The Genesis writer depicts this struggle in terms of the 'fruit of the tree of the knowledge of good and evil'. A more scientific 'handle' might suggest that the struggle is a consequence of the advent of 'mind', which itself is the result of significant growth in the size and the adaptability of the human brain. Each may be right in its own way, and we need not feel we have to choose between them. Each approach is trying, through its own language, to explore a deep mystery that we intuit within and among ourselves, but cannot explain.

Let's just pause for a gentle stroll through the centuries – and especially through the decades of our own lifetimes, to notice what these two 'branches' are actually doing.

To see this with any degree of clarity we first have to take off the dark glasses that most of us wear, that tend to distort our vision and make us see only the bad news. Even those who have not been explicitly taught to regard themselves as 'sinners' still have a strong sense of how much is wrong in our world and our societies. It's not hard to see what the 'bad branch' is doing.

The 'bad branch', we might say, grows with every self-focused choice that any of us makes (including our choices not to choose the better way in any given situation). It also thrives on every bit of negative energy we feed into the atmosphere around us – every sarcastic word, every thoughtless criticism, every grouch and grumble. So we can see, if we dare to look, how this 'knowledge of evil' has grown apace, from our early ancestors' choices to take their own advantage at the expense of the tribe, to our present condition, where global war is an ever-present threat, and where our streets and homes are constantly harrowed by quarrels, betrayals, violence in word and deed, and the kind of greed that blinds us to the abject poverty of one-sixth of the world's people. The consumer mentality, and the subtle, invisible machinations of multinational corporations damage us all in ways against which there seems to be no defence, while all the while we live our lives in wariness of the mugger, the terrorist alert, the computer virus, and a thousand other threats.

The escalation of the downward drag of 'evil' leads rapidly in Genesis from an act of disobedience by our 'first parents' to an act of murder by their offspring Cain, who kills his brother Abel in a fit of envy. Though the writer couldn't have known it consciously, he was warning of the power of fear and greed to sabotage the process of humanisation. The baggage of wrong-choosing has already grown from molehill to mountain in just one 'generation', in the Genesis story. And now, millions of generations after the first dawn of consciousness, each of us is born into a situation where we will have to carry our own share of the *cumulative* effects of all this wrong (self-focused) choosing and acting that has shaped our development since we first became creatures endowed with mind.

However – and here comes the good news – the 'good branch' has been growing too through the ages, and this is something we often overlook. When I think back to my own childhood, and the world I was growing up in, I notice some startling signs of how the 'good branch' has grown, even in such a relatively short period. For example …

Fifty years ago, nobody seriously questioned the need for war to resolve international disputes. Today there is a powerful swell of public opinion that challenges the very legitimacy of violent action to resolve any kind of problem. Violence in our classrooms and homes is outlawed, and state violence for political ends brings millions of ordinary citizens onto the streets in mass protest.

Today we see daily evidence of the commitment of our caring professions, and a public demand that they should be properly supported and rewarded in our society. It often amazes me just how much trouble ordinary folk will take to rescue a lost kitten, let alone another human being. We see, through global television and the internet, the devastating effects of world poverty, and we cannot remain unmoved. Actions such as Make Poverty History capture our collective imagination, and inspire our practical commitment. Appeals for aid, such as the Asian Tsunami appeal on a global scale, or local appeals like the BBC's annual Children in Need, yield huge sums of relief, from the donations of ordinary men and women. Global communications have opened our eyes, and our hearts.

Technical, scientific and medical progress has given us the possibility of longer and healthier lives, while those responsible for educating our young reveal tremendous dedication in devoting their energy and ability to the nurturing of the next generation. Ecologists, and those who are actively and practically concerned about the well-being of our planet have a voice today that was a mere whisper fifty years ago.

I could go on and on, but I would rather invite you to consider for yourself how the 'tree of the knowledge of good and evil' is looking to you, from where you are standing today in the twenty-first century. Just as we inherit the cumulative effect of our potential for harm, so too we each begin our lives with a rich legacy of everything good and life-giving that humankind has learned through the aeons. Almost every child born today will learn to walk and talk within a couple of years. It took humanity as a whole aeons of evolution to reach this level of ability. We take for granted the rapid acquisition of skills that our forebears took hundreds of generations to master. We expect, as of right, a level of health and education provision which only a few generations ago would have seemed like mere fantasy. All this we inherit. Truly, we stand on giants' shoulders!

How do you feel?
Has the 'bad branch' gone so completely out of control that it has taken over the whole show? Is the 'good branch' thriving or struggling'?
What can you do at a personal level to put your skills and energy into nourishing what is making us more human, and working against what is pulling us down into the less-than-human?

There is another twist to the tale. The two 'branches' have become hopelessly intertwined. We may do the right thing, but for seriously wrong reasons. We may do much that is wrong, but our intentions may be pure. And whatever we do and choose will be heavily influenced by the cumulative effects of all that has gone before, both for good and for ill.

Is it all going anywhere? We may feel that our own little efforts at becoming more human, our own contributions to aid appeals, our own attempts to be more caring, are totally overshadowed by the dark powers of selfishness that seem to underpin so much of what happens in our world.

Two little boys were comparing notes about how far they had progressed in their religious education classes. One boasted proudly: 'We're up to Original Sin!' To which the other retorted 'That's nothing! We're beyond Redemption!'

Are we up to original sin?

Are we beyond redemption?

More interesting questions might be:

Are we on our own with this desire to be more and more *human*?

Or is the universe itself striving with us towards the same goal?

Does the universe run on love, or doesn't it care a hoot about how we are and what becomes of us?

Let's investigate …

Does love really make the world go round?

We say, readily enough, that 'God is love'. Do we really believe it? Is it an empty and overused cliché. Or could it possibly be true?

Before we go on to consider some of the implications of committing ourselves to a 'contract with life' – a contract to work towards becoming more and more fully human, now might be a good moment to pause for another pair of big questions …

- Do you think the intelligence that guides the universe is benevolent (or merely neutral, or perhaps even hostile)? In short, does Life mean well with us?
- If you *do* feel and trust that the guiding principle of life is one of love and benevolence, why is there so much of the opposite around?

Most of us have grappled with questions like these from time to time, though we may have expressed them differently. There are no easy answers. Perhaps there are no answers at all. But there are some ways into these questions that it may be fruitful to explore. They are questions that profoundly affect our response to the invitation to enter into a 'contract with life'.

When I ask myself whether I believe the universe is ultimately held and guided in love, or whether it is simply neutral, or even hostile, I keep coming back to the overwhelming conviction that it is indeed held in love. My reasons for this conviction, however, are not because I have been taught to believe it. In fact, I actually had to let go of the 'taught certainties' almost completely, before I was free to discover for myself the deeper truth within them. I come to this conviction from my own felt, personal experience, and by asking myself these questions:

- When, in my life, have I felt what I might call 'the touch of God' – perhaps times when I felt especially blessed, or very close to creation or another person, or strangely guided to do what proved to be the most life-giving thing?
- As I recall such moments, how did I *feel*? Did I feel that I was in the hands of something life-giving and benevolent, or not?
- What fruits did these moments bear? Did they make any difference to

me, or to how I lived, or desired to live, from then on? Did they have any effect on other people? If so, did they help, or harm the people thus affected?

When I reflect like this, I can say without hesitation that such 'encounters with God' have always felt like being in touch with something overwhelmingly benevolent – something that is totally committed to bringing life from whatever circumstances arise, and constantly seeking to grow good fruit out of my own, usually deeply inadequate responses.

Research conducted by the Alister Hardy Institute in Oxford at the end of the twentieth century revealed that a surprisingly large number of people said that they had had spiritual experiences of this nature, which continued to affect the way they lived their lives and made their day-to-day decisions.

It appears I am not alone in my conviction that moments when we feel 'the touch of God' are overwhelmingly accompanied by a sense of being held in a universe that is not neutral, but is charged with a power and a presence of wisdom, goodness and love – a power that then in some small way affects our *own* presence in the world, if we choose to let it do so.

We see this very same commitment to life manifesting itself in every aspect of the evolution story. Life, it appears, will *not* be denied, come hell and high water, come extinctions and catastrophes. It keeps on going, and growing whatever befalls. We are looking at an unremitting drive for *life* here, whether in our physical evolution, or in the way our lives ultimately unfold. Life is quite extraordinarily persistent. If this is true at the physical level, does it not also hold at the level of our minds and our spirits?

But this leads us to the second of the questions. If this is so, why do we see so much around us, and within us, that appears to be working in the opposite direction? If it's true that the power of love makes the world go round, then what is it that keeps jamming the brakes on?

I have a candidate to bring to you as chief suspect: Fear!

A funny thing happens when we experience fear, or feel threatened in some way. When we still roamed the savannah, fear usually meant that a predator was approaching. All our instincts instantly activated the 'defence strategy'. Our bodies became acutely primed for 'fight or flight', whichever was the more expedient. The adrenalin kicked in, the muscles got set for action, and the ancient parts of the brain – the parts that control our instinctive responses and ensure our survival - took over the controls.

When the danger was constant, these responses became 'hard-wired'. They formed actual, permanent neural connections in our brains. This hard-wiring brought with it not just the instinct to fight or flee, but also the many convoluted strategies, which we (and indeed all of the animal kingdom) still use very skilfully, both to defend and to attack, such as deception, subterfuge, camouflage and withdrawal. The astounding ability of various occupants of the natural world, from tiny insects to lumbering quadrupeds, to inflict malicious damage on other creatures, going way beyond the needs of the next meal, should convince us that we are not alone in our propensity towards malevolence.

Fear, of course, is a necessary and basically healthy defence mechanism, warning us of danger and empowering us to protect ourselves and each other. But has it taken us over, like a rampant weed in an otherwise orderly garden?

Now, for human beings in the twenty-first century, the threat takes different forms. The prowling tiger is perhaps nothing more deadly than an aggressive manager, a domineering partner or the general negativity that is drip-fed into us day after day by the media. It doesn't matter – the effect is the same as it was when we were facing primal predators. The ancient part of the brain takes over, and temporarily overrides all the 'improvements' that nature has evolved and that make us potentially people who can reflect on life and meaning, and make choices either for or against the fullness of that life.

When our ancient (lower) brains register danger, even if that threat is nothing more than a suburban snub from the neighbours, we instinctively regress to the primal programming. Neuroscientists can actually tell us how the neural connections react in the process, and how if a negative response to life becomes habitual, we can, as it were, 'set' that way. If we do, it will be become impossible to make choices from any 'higher' place.

An aunt of mine used to tell me, when I was a child, that if I kept a grumpy expression on my face for too long, my face would 'set' that way, and I would have a permanent scowl. In a way, she was right. That seems to be very much the way our brains work when it comes to activating these primal survival mechanisms.

What are you most afraid of?
How does this affect the way you live and relate to others?
Try naming your fears, and maybe setting them down on paper. Put them 'out there' and look at them with the faculties of your 'higher brain' and the responses of your heart.
Look back over the events of the past week. Have you reacted to any situations using just the ancient survival mechanisms? Would you, on reflection, wish to have reacted differently?
Just notice how you feel.

The plea of self-defence

Our excuse for getting stuck in this lesser place, where fear rules, is the old favourite: self-defence. The most ancient layers of our brain are programmed to react as the predators of the savannah did: to defend ourselves against attack, and to attack other creatures in order to have something to eat. These are the facts, but if we believe that the intelligence of life is shaping those facts, then we can trust that there are other ways, largely still unexplored, to respond to life's challenges and choices.

If there can be said to be such a thing as 'original sin', surely it must have something to do with this patterning – a pattern that needs truly radical transformation if we are to be freed of it. Is this ancient programming just the way things are, or can it, in humankind, truly be regarded as the beginning of 'sin' - something that we have intentionally chosen?

Our cat, Jasper, catches baby rabbits in the spring and bites their heads off. I get upset every time. I even rail at the cat and tell him what a naughty creature he is. But of course he isn't any such thing. He is simply following his instinctual drives. He is a cat, and not a rational creature with the power of choice over his responses.

This is not true of ourselves. Like Jasper, we too have a deep and ancient layer of mind that reacts instinctively, either to take our 'prey' when we have the chance, or to bring in all the defence mechanisms when we are under threat. The big, big difference is that we also have higher layers of brain and mind, and with them, the potential to reflect on whether the instinctive response is really the most life-giving course to choose.

As we have already seen, the advent of mind brings not just the potential for good and evil, but, even more significantly, the *knowledge* of the potential for good and evil. What we may regard as malicious and even 'evil' in the animal kingdom is perpetrated in 'unknowing'. When it happens in the human domain it is perpetrated *knowingly*. This is the crucial development that gives our behaviour a moral loading and challenges us to be responsible for our choices.

The instincts don't go away, of course. Whenever danger lurks, stage one of our responses will always kick in, and we can't prevent it. But we don't have to run with it. We can deliberately choose to stop, count to ten, listen to our hearts, and *then* perhaps choose a different, and more measured course. As we proceed with our journey, we will explore some of the ways in which it might be possible to do so.

This instinct of reverting to the reptilian brain when we are under threat is one of the residual effects of an early layer of our evolution. We may call it 'sin', and we must indeed take responsibility for where it may lead us. But the advent of mind and rational self-awareness is also the dawn of something beyond our present horizon that could enable us to act not from our lower mind centre, but from something much higher – something that is still evolving. It is perhaps much more like a promise just emerging, than a condemnation for being, at present, so conditioned by these ancient survival instincts.

And fear is what causes these instinctual reactions to be activated. Tragically, when they are activated and, metaphorically speaking, our hackles go up and we are ready for the 'enemy', then that 'enemy' can very quickly become a real, and not just an imagined threat. There is a simple, inexorable logic, which we have all seen in action, whether in office politics, domestic rows or international stand-offs:

• We feel insecure in a particular situation
• We adopt a defensive pose to protect ourselves from exposure
• We counter any threatening comments or perceived criticism with immediate aggression
• The other people involved in the situation perceive these unconscious signals as a declaration of hostilities, and they react with a heightened degree of hostility themselves.
• The negative spiral has been activated, and is almost impossible to halt.

And it all boils down to fear.

> Fear, it seems to me, is the greatest enemy of love.
> And inappropriate fear is therefore inimical to life,
> Fear has the power to block the growth of life into its fullness.
> It has the power to freeze us into an immature stage of our evolution.
> Is this really how we want things to be?
> And, if not, how can we be freed to move beyond this deadlock?

The other side of this coin is 'greed'. To survive, we need to get our prey. To get our prey we have to be ruthless. We will either have to kill something to eat, or fight the competition for our bit of grazing space.

It can be truly alarming to reflect on how far these primal instincts still shape the way we are today.

The 'prey' now may be a better salary, a bigger house, a more power-ful car, a healthier bank balance, a higher status. These things are far beyond our survival needs, but we sometimes pursue them as though our life depended on them, sacrificing a great deal of value along the way (such as relationships, health, time to relax, or play, or simply to gaze at the sunset). In the context of modern living, the *needs* of the savannah have become hard-wired into what can only be called *greed*.

But if we can transcend our fears, perhaps we can transcend our greed, and move on into a future that is bigger, and greater, than anything we can currently imagine.

One more question, before we move on:

Which is more helpful, do you feel, in the quest to become ever more truly human: To beat down the 'lower brain' reactions, seeing them as 'sin' to be atoned for, and to punish ourselves and each other for their effects, or

To nourish the higher centres of thought in ourselves and in our society, so that, individually and collectively, we might begin to transcend the instinctive reactions that so often drive us?

If you came to the conclusion that the intelligence that guides the universe is motivated by love, which of these two possible approaches do you think that intelligence would favour?

Let's re-visit our first parents for a few moments, and see how they deal with their fears in this most celebrated of 'who-dunnits'.

Meet your inner serpent ...

Maybe Eve was right ... maybe it *was* the serpent's fault ...

Let's just join the proverbial fly on the wall and watch what happens after our early ancestors discover the joys, and the hazards, of the fruit of the tree of the knowledge of good and evil. Let's eavesdrop on the conversations that according to the writer of Genesis, ensue after humankind has become *homo sapiens* – creatures with the power of *mind*, and thus creatures who will forevermore face the challenge of choice in all their dealings.

The first significant comment comes from Adam:

> Yahweh God called to the man. 'Where are you?' he asked. 'I heard the sound of you in the garden,' he replied. 'I was afraid because I was naked, so I hid.' (Genesis 3:8)

I was afraid. I hid.

And we have been afraid, and we have been hiding ever since.

This begins to sound like a schoolboy drama: father says No! Children do it anyway. Father comes along the warpath. Children hide, are discovered, make their excuses and take their punishment. We can surely read Genesis like that, but if we do, what kind of a 'god' are we looking at? Is this the creator of trillions of galaxies, stirring in the tissues of our hearts and minds, prompting us always to reach for the very best within each of us, for the sake of all of us?

A closer look at the serpent's story has made me wonder whether perhaps the Genesis writer was unconsciously articulating a story of which he himself was only reading the topmost layer of meaning.

The psychology is spot on, of course. When we are afraid, we hide, and when we are caught, we throw the blame in any direction except back to ourselves. But is there more to this story than this?

Let's begin by looking at the immediate results of our ancestors' 'fall from grace'. Caught red-handed in the act of disobedience they use two well-worn techniques to get out of trouble – the Fig Leaf and the Blame Chain!

Their instant response to their predicament is to cover themselves up, because they realise that they are 'naked', that they are exposed and vulnerable. Can you imagine, perhaps, how it might have been, when our early forebears first stood upright on the savannah? There would have been advantages, of course – increased vision, for example, and the freedom to use our hands. But there would have been huge drawbacks too. And one of them would have been the fact of exposing our tender undercarriage to possible attack. Perhaps this was the beginning of our sense of nakedness, that the Genesis writer so vividly evokes. It might also have been the beginning of the illusion that we as human beings were somehow 'above' the rest of creation, and the start of a dangerously arrogant attitude towards our world.

The fig leaf becomes the symbol of all our subsequent attempts to cover ourselves. We wear all kinds of different masks to suit different needs and relationships. What we very rarely, if ever do, is reveal ourselves totally and without defences to any other human being. We all know how dangerous that would be. Most of our disguises are unconscious. Some are deliberate – for example when we seek an 'image makeover' or employ a 'spin doctor' to intentionally put a modified persona out into the world. In our times, 'image' has become very big business indeed, starting from our toddlers' demands for designer-label trainers to the glittering fog in which our world leaders often conceal themselves against honest scrutiny.

It's all very sophisticated and subtle now.

'The snake', we learn, in the Genesis imagery, 'was the most subtle of all the wild animals that Yahweh God had made' (Genesis 3:1).

If the Genesis serpent is in part at least the voice of our 'lower' (or reptilian!) brain, then we can readily see how subtle indeed are the movements in our minds that cause us to react as we do. We are afraid, and so we hide. Remember what happens in the brain when we feel threatened – we revert to the lower level of brain activity, which is focused on survival and little else. The inner serpent takes over, to manage the fear-inducing situation, and tells us to get out our fig leaves.

But if the masks don't work, and someone sees through us anyway, Plan B of the defence strategy is invoked – the 'blame chain'. It wasn't me! It was someone else's fault! And so Adam blames Eve and Eve blames the poor old serpent.

We blame someone else, and we have been blaming someone else ever since.

But maybe Eve was right, and it *was* a lot to do with the serpent. Maybe at a deeper layer of meaning, this Genesis story is actually about fear, and the effects of fear. When we live in fear, the inner serpent takes over the steering wheel. On come the fig leaves. Off fly the accusations. And in no time we are in the hall of mirrors.

Because this is about *projection*. What we don't like in ourselves (for example the fact that we have got something wrong, chosen the 'evil'

branch in a particular matter) we project out to some convenient
'other' – a colleague, a partner, the government, or maybe an unfortunate
minority group in our society. It's their fault. We can dismiss the problem,
and if necessary we will even collude in the final removal of the chosen
scapegoat, as all our warmongering testifies. Of course, if we do get rid of
the scapegoat upon whom we have loaded our own wrong-choosing and
wrongdoing, we will soon need to find a new one, so that the blame chain
remains intact for the next time we need it.

I have lived in Germany, and been very impressed by the commitment
of the present generation of the German people to peace, and their
horror of anything military. This is a very obvious reaction to their recent
history. When questions of war arise, as they have done in our present
times, the German people (and others, of course) are in very vocal oppo-
sition. This has made me wonder why it is that they have apparently
learned from their parents' mistakes, and we have not. Then a possible
answer dawned on me.

At the end of the Second World War, the German people (many of
whom offered courageous resistance to the Nazi regime) quite simply
had no one they could blame for the events that led to the physical and
moral devastation of their land. The nations on the 'winning' side,
however, have missed out on this learning opportunity, because they were
able to project all the uncomfortable questions out to the 'losers' and
avoid looking at their own part in the catastrophe. I have come to the
conclusion that we only ever learn from our mistakes if and when we
honestly acknowledge that they are *our* mistakes, and not someone else's.

The 'winner', of course, invariably gets to write the history books, and so
the apparently 'successful' pattern of using the reptilian brain to make
decisions, and projecting any failure, especially moral failure, out onto
someone else (usually the 'losers'), becomes hard-wired in the human
psyche.

But mirrors don't just reflect the bad. They reflect our glory too. And
thereby hangs a tale.

Just suppose that we are not only projecting our 'bad stuff' outwards,
but our 'good stuff' too. Marianne Williamson (though the quote is often
attributed to Nelson Mandela), in her book *Return to Love,* writes:

> *Our deepest fear is not that we are inadequate.*
> *Our deepest fear is that we are powerful beyond measure.*
> *It is our light, not our darkness, that frightens us.*

What a thought! It raises a big question in my mind:

If we are so afraid of who we might have the potential to become – a species beyond homo sapiens even – a humanity with the potential to engage with divinity, have we projected this potential outwards too?
Have we projected it onto an image of God?
An image of God like that in Genesis, of the controlling father who keeps us infantile and stops us growing up?

To suggest that we have projected the greatness of our own potential on to an 'out-there God' isn't, of course, the same as suggesting that there is no God at all. It is only to say that our own human images of 'God' will inevitably fall a long, long way short of the reality of the power that is 'the intelligence and wisdom of all life', who is quietly calling us, moment by moment, to grow towards our destiny.

Our defensive reactions can freeze us into spiritual infancy.

Are we going to let an outgrown image of 'God' get away with that?

And, most subtle and scary of all, if the Genesis serpent is the voice of our lower brain, urging us to grow into the fullness of our humanity – even if the next stage inevitably brings us up against the constant challenge of choice between good and evil – if the serpent is saying 'I'm a reptile and will always be a reptile, but you have the potential to rise to a more highly-evolved state than this, though the cost will be the challenge of choice, and the need to think again about your image of who or what God really is', then ...

Did the serpent have a point? Was he doing us a favour when he nudged us towards the next stage of our Becoming. And is fear the real villain of the piece? Fear of our potential to choose the harmful ways, and an even greater fear of growing into a greatness and a glory we cannot even imagine, if only there were someone to show us how.

Yes, if only there were someone to show us how.

Because good will and good intentions won't cut it on their own. We simply can't move on on our own. We need someone to lead the way ...

Who will show us how?

The evolution story reveals a clue to this 'moving on'. We need help with it. In fact we are as *helpless* to do it alone as a newborn child is helpless to grow to maturity in its own power alone. As we reflect on the Brain Story, we discover a very interesting fact. In its higher stages of evolution, the development of our mind requires a *model*.

This occurs at a personal level, as we mature from infancy to adulthood. We learn to walk by being shown the skill, and allowed the freedom to practise it. We learn speech from those who have already mastered language and encourage us to use it. We learn ways of relating to others from those who are themselves in mature relationship with others. The quality of the model is crucial, and this fact underpins a great deal of child psychology. A child with poor role models is at serious risk of impaired mental and emotional development.

> *'Someone who is fully able to do something or behave in a certain way must perform the role of model if a similar ability is to be awakened in the child'*
> (Joseph Chilton Pearce, *The Biology of Transcendence*).

This latest stage of becoming human, and developing more truly human patterns of thought and behaviour, needs the model of someone who has already achieved that greater fullness of their humanity.

In the process of individual development, the model (usually the person caring for the child) actually carries out the higher brain functions for the child until the necessary growth has taken place and the child can move towards independence. So, for example, we curb the tendencies of small children to live by the law of the jungle, and we model an example of civility for them until they become capable of reflecting for themselves and, hopefully, choosing the better paths. And to choose those better paths, they need the right models. And, as we know, they learn best from who, and how, we are, not just from what we say. This is very much an example–driven learning curve.

What is true for each of us in our personal development is surely also true for all of us, as we evolve into a species that is more and more fully human. We need a model …

But who will show us how?

The answer lies readily accessible in our history and in the sacred traditions of the world. From time to time true leaders and models emerge from among us. They are people who seem to be already living at a higher state of evolution than we are ourselves. How we react to such people varies enormously and seems to reflect the degree of trust or fear that dominates our hearts. To the extent that we are driven largely by fear, and the defence/attack reflexes of the instinctual part of our brain, we may deride and destroy such models. There is a long tradition of doing exactly that. But if we allow our higher brain functions to have a say in the matter, we may realise just what a gift – what an essential link to future possibility beyond our imagining – such people truly are, and we will actively seek them out.

However we react, we know in our hearts that these men and women are really living out what it means to be fully human to a much greater extent than we ourselves are, as yet, capable of doing. For Christians, one model in particular has become the apex of *all* that it means to be *fully* human, and we will explore his story shortly, as the crucial key to our own story and the world's story.

So what's to learn from this brief trip into neurobiology?

First, 'becoming human' leads to the flowering of creative imagination, the ability to bring to mind infinite possibilities and to choose to make them real.

Second, 'becoming human' needs a model – someone who is already living a more fully evolved life, and who awakens its possibilities in us.

Third, everything is built on what went before. The lower brain isn't thrown out in favour of a newer model, but each new development incorporates the features of what was there before, in order to evolve a more highly developed brain. The same may be true for all our experience. Nothing is wasted. Everything contributes to our Becoming. All of our past, both individual and collective, is part of our future.

Finally, there is a constant danger that, when we feel threatened, we tend to go back to focusing our choices and actions on the ancient imprints in our lower, more primitive, brain – that is, we shoot from the hip, become defensive, and fail to act out of our creative potential and higher levels of sensitivity. If the state of fear is endemic (as it is in our Western culture today), then this regression could become so ingrained that it shapes our whole lives and our whole culture. In other words, *fear* is a real killer, and may be the biggest threat to our ongoing quest to become more and more fully human.

We will return to these thoughts when we come to reflect on who our model is and what that model has to say about fear.

As you look back over your own story, who has modelled for you a better way of being human? For all of us, the prime model in infancy is our mother or surrogate care-giver. As we grow up, other people also act as role models for us, awakening in us a desire to be more like them in particular aspects of our living. Who are the human role models you cherish? What aspects of being human did/do they model for you?

No way back

When our hapless forebears left the comfort zone of Eden, or, less figuratively, when we evolved beyond the state of being creatures of instinct, to become creatures with mind and choice and reflective awareness, the Genesis writer presents this as a catastrophe, and the beginning of the end:

> So Yahweh God expelled him from the garden of Eden, to till the soil from which he had been taken. He banished the man, and in front of the garden of Eden he posted the great winged creatures and the fiery flashing sword, to guard the way to the tree of life. (Genesis 3:24)

This is a pretty unequivocal road block! It reads, in the boldest of letters: 'No Way Back'. The sword that comes down to cut off any possibility of a retreat into pre-rational stages of evolution raises once again the question, 'Is this punishment or progress?' Is it a banishment from something good, or is it a logical statement of fact: there is no way back. A child, once born, can never go back into the prenatal comfort zone of its mother's womb.

Whether we see this great threshold experience as the beginning of the end, or the end of the beginning, makes a very big difference to our understanding of our relationship with God and our quest to 'become human'.

If it is the beginning of the end, we need rescuing. We need a saviour. Our theology will be focused *backwards*, and that saviour will come to restore us to how we were (before we messed it all up).

If it is the end of the beginning, we still need help – big time. Not because we are lost, but because we are immature – unripe – far from being fully human. Our theology will be focused *forwards*. We need a model who will lead us forward into all we might become, all that the fullness of 'God's dream' for humanity has yet to reveal, whatever that moving forward may cost.

So we stand on this threshold, asking ourselves …

Did we 'fall' backwards or forwards?
Are we standing at the beginning of the end, or the end of the beginning?
Do we need a saviour who rescues us or a model who leads us forwards?

Which direction works for you?

If you feel that we have reached the beginning of the end, this may be as far as this book will go for you.

If you feel we are standing at the end of the beginning, then take heart, and journey on …

THE HINGE OF HISTORY

'*Give me a lever long enough and a place to stand and I will move the world.*'

Archimedes

When the pilgrim is ready, the guide appears ...

Our much-needed model is like this proverbial guide. The wisdom of the saying suggests that when we are ready to learn, a teacher will be forthcoming. When we are ready to move on, into uncharted terrain, the guide will appear.

The guide is the one who will reveal the way from our present state of being (*homo sapiens*) to whatever shall follow after. The words of Archimedes caught my attention because they speak of two things that this guide needs to do the job – the *lever*, and the *right place to stand*, in order to move the world.

Archimedes was obviously thinking of mechanical principles, and how long a lever would need to be in order to shift a mass as large as planet Earth, and where one would have to be located oneself, in order to operate this kind of leverage. He might have concluded that the length of the lever would be astronomical, and the person operating it would be perched somewhere in deep space.

When I reflect on this analogy, however, I have a radically different image of the kind of lever that could move us beyond where we are, towards whatever it means to be a fully evolved human being.

Such a lever, I suggest, wouldn't be anything like what we have known so far – it wouldn't be the leverage of wealth or brute force, political power, clever intellect or flawless physique. We have tried all of these, and nothing has shifted us an inch out of our accustomed orbit. None of these could move the human race into a different trajectory. No, it would be something so quiet and unassuming, you would only find it if you really searched, only hear it if you could learn to listen to the sound of silence, and it would most likely not be in any of the obvious places. It would be love.

And where would the person operating this lever have to stand?

Not out in deep space, I suggest. But right here in the thick of it all, in the mess and the muddle of all that it means to be a partially evolved, still very incomplete and chaotic human family.

So during this stage of our quest, we will explore what this lever really means in practice, who is operating it for us, and what is likely to happen to the world as a result.

An unlikely candidate

There's nothing new about finding what you most need and desire in the very last place you expected to look for it.

The great leaders of humankind have frequently emerged out of the most unpromising of situations, and been the least likely candidates for such a role. Nelson Mandela, the first president of a free and democratic South Africa, emerged out of years of imprisonment and exile on Robben Island, just, it seems, when the time was right for radical change.

Oscar Romero, who fearlessly championed the cause of the oppressed in South America, emerged out of a conventional and traditional church system that resisted any challenge to embrace the radical poverty of the Christian gospel. He experienced his own awakening, and went on to call to wakefulness all those who held unjust power around him, just when the time was right for change in Latin America.

But in this quest, we will be exploring the vision of one particular unlikely candidate whom I bring to you as the model we are seeking to lead us beyond ourselves using the lever of love – a man called Jesus, raised in the Galilean town of Nazareth, around two thousand years ago.

On a backpacking trip to Israel, I was struck – and amused – by the fact that the name Jesus, and its Arab version Issa, is extremely common in that part of the world. As for Nazareth, apparently it was considered completely beyond the pale in Jesus' day, certainly not at all a place from which a prophet – let alone a Messiah – would ever emerge. Jesus' life begins, and ends, by flying in the face of expectations and assumptions. We can expect it to do something similar to our own expectations and assumptions. Don't imagine that he is going to tuck us up in our comfort blankets.

Tradition has wrapped his obscure beginnings in colourful robes, and perhaps we will never know – or need to know – exactly how he came to birth, in a remote village in the Middle East, two thousand years ago. Of much greater interest is what this story *means*. We know him, very well, as 'the babe in the manger', but who is this man, this most radical of leaders? Who was he really? And what does his life mean?

You will notice that the word 'radical' crops up again and again as we stand at this crossroads of our journey. 'Radical' means 'coming up from the roots'. We have reflected on our roots, and on everything that has led us on our quest to become human, both at the level of our physical being, and of our rational powers. But now those roots are poised to become wings. And a little child in a hidden corner of the world is going to be the key to this transformation. He is going to move the world. His lever will be love, and to use it, he needs to stand right here in the midst of us.

But we are running ahead of ourselves:

- If this child is the Guide we are waiting for, why was two thousand years ago the right moment for his appearance, and where did he come from?
- Did he 'drop from heaven', at an apparently arbitrary moment in human history, or did he emerge out of our lived human story when the time was right?
- What are we to make of him, and how are we to relate to him? Who *is* he, and what does his story mean?

Is he just another pious myth, or is he really the hinge of history?

Awakening

Many paths open up to us if we explore the question 'Why *then?*'

Why, in the course of fifteen billion years of the existence of our universe, why in the course of at least 100,000 years of the existence on earth of *homo sapiens*, why was two thousand years ago the right time for a breakthrough into a new dimension in the quest for what it means to 'become human'?

The slow but steady journey of the human heart towards spiritual awakening is something – literally – of a mystery tour. Gradually, through the many millennia that precede our own, history is slowly changing gear. No longer merely physical and rational beings, we are evolving into a new dimension of our destiny – the spiritual ...

We can only hope to make a whistle-stop tour of the evolving sense of mystery and self-reflectiveness, which we all inherit from our ancient forebears, but the tour is worth the trouble.

Our first port of call might be southern France, around 30,000 years ago. This is the domain of the cave painters – distant ancestors of ours, who adorned the walls of their caves with remarkable images of the animals they hunted and the natural world around them. No big deal, you might say. We do this all the time, only now we do it with camcorders and multi-media displays. The interesting thing about the cave paintings is that they are the earliest evidence of human beings who are reflecting on their place in the scheme of things, expressing their response, and revealing that most precious gift of the creating wisdom to the created realm – *creativity*.

Far from France, deep in the deserts of central Australia, I have gazed myself, in silent wonder, on ancient paintings on the walls of caves in the heart of the great monolith Uluru. Here, it is thought, the Anangu tribe have occupied the region for at least 12,000 years. Today, the descendants of these aboriginal artists are more than willing to share something of their spiritual heritage with those who come seeking with an open heart. They will tell you the stories they tell their own children, about the many sacred secrets of the 'dreamtime', locked into that massive rock. They will ask you to respect its sacredness and the encounter will change something inside of you, if you let it.

Another pathway of discovery leads us back to northern climes. The time? Approximately five thousand years ago. The place? County Meath in Ireland. There we discover several large mounds, which on investigation are revealed to be cairns containing passages and burial chambers, dating from about 3250 to 3000 BC. Some of them appear to be merely ancient, overgrown mounds. But those mounds contain a powerful secret.

One of the best known of these burial chambers is at Newgrange. If you want an experience of enlightenment, the place to be is in the central chamber at Newgrange at dawn on the day of the winter solstice. At that moment, and at no other, an amazing event takes place. The rising sun penetrates a small aperture, to flood the innermost chamber with light.

Five thousand years ago, therefore, humankind was making connections between the perceived movements of the earth relative to sun and stars, and reaching out to connect to these mysteries in a tangible way. It is no accident that the solstice dawnlight brings a deep inner chamber to glorious light. The cairns are designed to focus on this mystery, and to celebrate it.

To find other dramatic burial chambers, we might venture further south to Egypt and her famous pyramids. The first pyramid complex dates from 2640 BC, and like the Irish cairns, the pyramids were clearly designed and built as burial chambers. But like the Irish chambers, these burial sites too may hold other secrets. One strong suggestion is that the layout of the pyramids is aligned to certain significant constellations of the night sky. Certainly, most of the pyramids are aligned to the cardinal points of the compass, with extraordinary accuracy. While the mathematics of this enterprise might well astound us, its spiritual significance may be even greater. In Egypt, over four thousand years ago, humankind was 'reaching for the stars', and seeking to make tangible connections between the Earth we live on and the mystery of the heavens around us.

It's a long road, that begins at least 30,000 years ago, but what does it reveal?

In my mind there is no doubt that this trail, on which we have stopped at just a few vantage points where the view is especially clear, is leading to a more and more explicit awareness of the mystery that surrounds all human life – a mystery that, with the advent of organised religion, some four thousand years ago, would be named, in English, 'God', and in all the names that humankind uses, to express a sense of the divine.

It reveals how human beings are expressing a growing awareness of this 'otherworld', this invisible mystery, through their creativity, through their sense of the importance of burying their dead with due ceremony, through their awareness of the sacredness of particular places, and their desire to focus their hearts and their senses on the powerful interplay between the here-and-now and the 'beyond'.

Humankind is becoming spiritually aware. There is a potent change brewing. And this new dimension of being human seems to be accelerating.

Thirty thousand years ago, we were discovering our creativity, on the cave walls of southern France.

Twelve thousand years ago we were aware of sacred place, and the 'dreamtime' in which our brief life on earth is connected to all that has gone before and will follow after – an awareness that reflects our first inklings of moral and spiritual responsibility.

Five thousand years ago we were seeking to express our sense of the eternal inter-relationship between the seen and the unseen worlds, the earth and the stars and the sun, and the power that holds all of these in being.

Four thousand years ago, we were formulating the first beginnings of organised religion, a process that would lead to the breakthrough moment of awareness that ...

This mystery is not only the source of all creation, but ...

This mystery is lovingly and intimately involved in what happens on planet Earth, and ...

This mystery actively wants humankind to be in right relationship with it, so that we might evolve into the fullness of our destiny.

When the pilgrim is ready the guide appears.

The pilgrim is the human family in its entirety.

The pilgrim is *homo sapiens*. Is the pilgrim ready? The events of two thousand years ago seem to say, 'Yes! And here is the Guide!'

Growing season

Springtime comes in many different guises.

I laughed when my friend in Queensland called me out into her garden in August to admire the first snowdrops peeping through the soil. Then I remembered that August in Queensland is the middle of winter, in spite of the 'Mediterranean' sunshine and the easy warmth.

In Ontario, on the banks of the Ottawa River, springtime comes in May. The woodland bursts into bloom with the delicate trilliums, the water reverberates with the song of the loons and in the city of Ottawa the tulips, donated to the city's people by the Queen of the Netherlands in gratitude for their hospitality to her in time of war, take over every green space and turn the city into a riot of colour.

In my own garden, spring reaches its high point in March, when the daffodils come again ... And it was as I was wandering through the garden one morning in March, that I found myself thinking exactly that: 'The daffodils have come again.' And then the ludicrousness of my unspoken comment hit me between the eyes. 'The daffodils have always been there', I corrected myself. 'You planted them there yourself many years ago. They haven't been anywhere else, so how can they have "come again"?' 'OK,' I conceded to myself, 'so they haven't been away, and they haven't "come again", but they have *revealed* themselves in a new way, now that springtime is here. They have revealed the daffodil-ness of them-selves. Until now they have been hidden away in the soil, waiting for the time to reveal what they are.'

Before you give up on this bizarre conversation going on inside myself, let me say in my defence that it wasn't as pointless as it may seem. Because for some time I had been struggling with the familiar phrase and received wisdom that, two thousand years ago, 'God came down to earth from heaven'. Something about it didn't ring true. How could God 'come down' to earth when surely God is ever-present in God's creation, and not some 'up there, out there' being who suddenly 'descends', as if on a state visit to the created world.

The fact is, of course, that these images originate in a cosmology that doesn't work for us today. We no longer think of God as 'up there' and earth as 'down here'. We have a very different understanding of our universe than our ancestors had, but our theology is slow to catch up. So how do the daffodils help to bring enlightenment?

Well, that morning the daffodils helped me grope my way towards a rather different understanding of what may have happened two thousand years ago.

The daffodils (and the snowdrops and the trilliums and tulips) are always there in the earth, but they reveal themselves in a special way in the springtime. Perhaps God too, always present in God's creation, *reveals* 'Godself' in a special way in a particular person born two thousand years ago.

The daffodils reveal themselves in springtime because the conditions are right. The temperature is rising and the level of solar energy is increasing. The conditions are right for a whole new season of growth. Does God, too, reveal 'Godself' when the time is right – when the human family has reached a level of spiritual awareness that makes us potentially open to a new revelation of what it means to be a fully evolved human being?

When the first daffodil opens its golden flower, soon there will be many many more. The garden will be alive with them, the forests will be carpeted with trilliums and bluebells, Ottawa will become one huge tulip festival. Jesus told his friends that he was the first of many brothers and sisters, and that others would soon do what he did, and much more besides. He was the first harbinger of a new spiritual springtime.

The daffodils herald the coming of the season when everything in the garden will come to its own flowering and fruitfulness. When God emerges from the earth, from the depths of a still-sleeping-but-just-awakening humanity, in the body, mind and soul of a baby born to an ordinary girl in the Middle East, a wake-up call quivers through all creation. This is a *radical* call – one that has its roots firmly in the earth, but its wings poised for flight.

The human adventure is changing gear.

After my conversation with the daffodils that morning something shifted inside me too. I wanted to proclaim that God doesn't come *down*, God comes *up*! God is less like a comet that suddenly sweeps into our orbit from outer space, and more like a tiny seed of possibility that can grow into a universe, and is gestating in the same soil that gives birth to *us*.

But this isn't just about substituting one preposition for another by playing around with the language we use. This, for me at least, was a serious and major shift of focus. It freed me to let go of what had become an outdated and unhelpful image of a God who descends to earth as a visiting alien, and engage instead with a human person who is so fully in tune with the wisdom and the love of the universe, so fired by the life of God, that he would become known to many as the Son of God (though he himself preferred to be known as 'the son of Man').

Does God come down or up?
Does God descend into our midst in the life of Jesus of Nazareth, as one who comes to us from outside and beyond ourselves, or does the wisdom and the love of God emerge among us when the time is right, revealing itself in a new and world-changing way in the person of Jesus of Nazareth?
What do you feel?

The future is announced

And so, in the fullness of time, One emerges from among us, who reveals what the 'human being, fully alive' will look like, and who embodies the values and attitudes that will make us fully human, if we only dare to take him, and his wisdom, his living and his dying, seriously. This is the lever that will move the world, and his chosen place to stand is right in the midst of life on planet Earth.

This is about *transformation*, not damage repair. We may have become a little fixated on a view of Jesus of Nazareth as a kind of supernatural visitor to our planet, who puts the clock back, and sets right all that went wrong from the beginning of our existence on earth. But suppose Jesus isn't about putting the clock *back*, but turning it *forward*, to give us a glimpse of everything that we ourselves might become, if we will take into our own lives and hearts the message that he brings, and the divinity that he embodies in his own living. And, paradoxically, the only time and place where the seed of that 'future' is to be found is in the present moment and the place where we are. The lever of love is operated from precisely *here* and exactly *now*.

Just suppose that God has, through all eternity, been brooding over this possibility, just as the Genesis writer suggests:

> Now the earth was a formless void, there was darkness over the deep, and God's Spirit hovered over the water. (Genesis 1:1)

Let's just stay awhile with this brooding Spirit here in this present moment, and see what else is going on in this mysterious interplay between the visible and the invisible worlds. And to make our reflection real, and earthed and grounded, we will allow that creative spirit to hover over the unfathomed depths in *ourselves,* just as we are, and where we are …

A prayer I often use to help me come to stillness is the Celtic-style invocation asking God to 'weave a stillness around my body, my mind and my heart'. You might like to share, in your own way, in a little meditation that can arise from this prayer.

Let yourself relax, and perhaps imagine God as a spinner, spinning Godself around the single fertilised cell who is you in your earthly beginnings. Watch as God weaves the cells and tissues into form and shape around that cell, in a deeply personal and loving way – as if you really matter! See God, the source of all creating wisdom, organising cells into organs, growing organs into interconnectedness, spinning your arteries, veins and capillaries into an intricate system of highways and byways, to make sure that not a single nook or cranny of you misses out on the food and oxygen it needs for life. Watch God spinning your skin and hair and fingernails to enclose and protect that tiny body and skeleton God has shaped and formed from that first cell.

Now move to consider the miracle of your mind. Perhaps God seems more like an embroiderer now. I remember how skilled my own mother was in the art of embroidery and how I so often watched her at work. 'God the Embroiderer' is about making connections – interweaving fibres of infinite colours, linking two points, again and again into a living network that will reveal a picture. God 'embroiders' the neural connections in your brain, and together these neural connections shape a unique mind – *your* mind. My mother embroidered by carefully placing connections of coloured thread in exactly the right positions. God takes the multi-coloured fibres of your unique and personal experience and places them in exactly the right positions to shape your mind. But my mother's embroidery, though beautiful, was static. God's embroidery is dynamic. It lives and grows and changes day by day, under the influence of every new experience and impression. God, surely, knows what this mind, in God's hands and God's time, can become – a reflection of God's own mind, a reflection of the deep web of wisdom that holds all creation in being.

And finally, contemplate the wonder of your spirit – the profound secret self of who you eternally are, known only to God. Imagine God weaving a cocoon in which your spirit may become prepared for transformation. Imagine God the nest-maker, preparing soul space in which your embryonic spirit may grow in the shelter and the warmth of God's brooding Spirit, calling your own into the fullness of life.

And so, God spins material form around the single cell of your beginning. God embroiders the neural connections that shape your mind, using the coloured fibres of your own experience and of the ancient human story whose imprint and memory you carry. And God shapes the space that holds your 'egg', the nest of your becoming, until you are ready to hatch into eternity.

God's dream unfolds as we reflect upon it. God's dream that draws humankind first through its physical evolution, then through the evolution of mind, and finally into the place of transcendence, in which our living spirit comes to self-awareness, and to the threshold of the potential to go beyond all we now call *homo sapiens*. And as God does this for humankind as a whole, and for each of us personally, so too does God's spirit hover over one in whom that fullness of humanity is complete – and therefore divine!

This is the one who comes *up* from among us, exactly when the human story is ready to receive him – the fully enlightened one – the one who lives completely true to the divine source whom he calls 'abba'.

Spinnning, embroidering, weaving, brooding – you will notice that these are very feminine images, and I make no apology for that. Because this mysterious process that exists from the beginning, and is coming to a pivotal moment in the birth of Jesus of Nazareth, is very much about bringing a new creation to birth. We are all invited to be a part of this birthing – it's not a gender issue!

What might this new creation be? Some distant heaven, for which we are going to need special visas, stamped with all our good works, or a visa-waiver form, granted by grace alone, that will steer us safely through the divine immigration channels? I think not. The new creation, I suggest, is our very own future as living beings in a universe whose guiding wisdom is love. It is the next, and maybe the final stage of our 'humanisation', and we are invited to shape that future ourselves, through our own choices and decisions and relationships with one another, guided by One who embodies that guiding wisdom of love in his every thought and deed.

And when this future is fully formed, we may be surprised to discover that it is heaven – and astounded at how little we guessed of the reality of it. I hope we will have reason to laugh at how all our guesses sold it way too short, at how we limited it to the narrow confines of our own immature minds and hearts, and above all, at how we presumed to decide that some of us should enter it and others not!

But to shape this future we are going to need a great deal of help. And maybe that's what we mean by that peculiarly Christian word 'grace'. Attempting to give birth to the new creation on our own is like trying to drive a car with an empty tank. 'Grace' is the fuel that goes in the tank, and the only source of that fuel is the source of life itself – the one Jesus calls 'abba', the alpha and the omega of creation.

Take a few moments of stillness to reflect on how you, personally, have been woven in the womb, how your mind has been shaped by the 'embroiderer' of your neural connections, and how your embryonic spirit rests in the cocoon of all that shall be, as the source of your life broods over it like a mother bird, coaxing it into its own, still unimaginable future.

Now might be a good point to adjust your watch to a new time zone – the FUTURE. Your own future. The future of humanity. The future of planet Earth. The model is poised to show us the way, and to empower us for the journey …

God's seedbed

The image of a seed is a good metaphor to help us direct our eyes and hearts towards the future. The one who will use the lever of love to shift the human family into a new relationship with God and with all creation, has chosen his place to stand in order to do the job: not out in deep space, but right here in the soil and the toil of human life on this planet. The seed is sown quietly and unobtrusively, and grows unrecognised, until the time is right.

The hinge of history opens the door into God's seedbed – the space of grace and love where all may come to ripeness.

Once, many moons ago, on a backpacking trek through Israel, we came upon fresh dates, straight from the date palm, on sale in the fruit market. Delighted at this coup, we bought a stem of the bright yellow fruit, relishing the prospect of eating fresh dates straight from the tree. We took just one bite of one of them, and then spat it out, disgusted by the bitter taste. But not wanting to throw them away, we stowed them in a plastic bag at the bottom of a backpack. Three weeks later, when we arrived at the airport to fly home, we discovered this plastic bag among the socks and the towels. By now the dates had lost their lovely golden colour and turned into a squashed brown sticky mess. Sadly we extracted them from the bottom of the backpack, and peeled off the plastic bag. One tentative bite, just for old time's sake, before we discarded them – and ... they were absolutely delicious! Nobody had told us you have to let dates ripen before you eat them, and that they actually have to go brown and sticky before they are fit to eat.

What if human beings are like dates. What we see now of our human condition is the bright yellow fruit straight from the palm, that thinks it's the bees' knees, and nothing can ever get better, but when you try living with it, you realise how bitter it can be, and you think the only thing to do with it is to spit it out. The Good News is: God who made us doesn't spit us out, just because we are still unripe. God lets us reach maturity. Maybe as a human family right now we are only about 5 per cent along the way to this maturity – this fullness of all we have the potential to become. But God will wait. And meanwhile God draws from among us the one who is already perfectly ripe and fully human. And in our ignorance and pride, we might very easily just discard him, as once we nearly discarded those ripened dates at the bottom of our backpacks.

I understand that the Aramaic word which is commonly translated as 'sin' can also mean 'unripeness'. Perhaps the present state of the human family is more 'unripe' than 'fallen'. How would you feel about this?

I have other reasons, too, for remembering that backpacking trip. We had planned it well in advance, and bought our flight tickets, only to discover three weeks before take-off that I was pregnant. At the risk of providing too much information, I can reveal that August in the Middle East, hiking and camping, is not the best backdrop for the early weeks of a first pregnancy. On several mornings I was quite sick, and I managed to go into a dead faint one day in the ancient temple precincts in Jerusalem, definitely for physiological, and not spiritual reasons.

For all its rose-tinted aura, pregnancy, especially in the early weeks, is not a bed of roses. There are times when you wish you'd never had the idea. But if all goes well, the day comes when a new marvel of humanity lies in your arms, and then you know why you did.

What if that's where we are now? In the early stages of bringing the new creation to birth? That might explain some of the pain and sickness and fear that bedevils our human communities.

Before we leave the Holy Land, perhaps I can share with you another, less happy aspect of the journey. We were camping in a little place near Magdala, and it happened to be the Day of Atonement (Yom Kippur), during which, we learned, nothing might be bought or sold, and no-one must be in transit on the roads, either on foot or by any other mode of transport. To our horror we discovered that the sales prohibition also included water, and that we were going to have to stay in our little tent all day without any. As the morning advanced, our tent turned into a tandoori oven and I was feeling really groggy. In desperation we set off to find some water, and persuaded a local Palestinian to let us have some. Like Jesus before him, this man broke the rules to help us in our need and we broke the rules ourselves, by walking the roads on the holy day. We broke the rules because the call of life was more insistent.

When I think of this incident, I think of the unripe dates too. I think of how we are just beginners – all of us – on this journey towards our full humanisation. I remember with thankfulness the good man who gave me fresh water that day, and I remember how Jesus repeatedly stressed that the calls of love take priority over the strict demands of the law.

We all needed watering that day. We were thirsty ourselves, and that which was still unborn within us (in my case literally, as well as spiritually) was thirsty. And when the water was given, we all grew. We all need watering all the time, and the wisdom of life is always longing to sustain and enrich all life, including the life that is still curled up like a seed, trying to come to birth in our hearts.

Imagine a simple seed packet. If you have one to hand, just hold it, and spend a little time with it. It probably has a brightly coloured picture on it of what the seeds inside will be when they come to the fullness of their life. Maybe it was this picture that enticed you to buy the seed packet in the first place.

On the back of the packet there will be the instructions for planting the seeds – where they should go, and how far apart, and in what kind of soil and season of the year. They are certainly not going to do anything at all as long as they remain inside the seed packet.

Now imagine the seeds themselves. They don't look even remotely like the picture on the packet. If you didn't know about seeds, and how they grow into something wildly different, you would think you had been taken for a ride by the seed merchant. You might just throw them away and cut your losses. But you *do* know about seeds. You *do* know they grow into something very different. And you know it takes *time*. On the basis of this knowledge, you dig a hole in the ground and bury them! Then you wait, in hope and in faith, for the day when they will reveal themselves for what they truly are.

When that day comes, the revelation of the fullness of the plant and the flower will show up the picture on the packet for what it is – just a two-dimensional impression of all that is to come, just something to get your juices flowing and persuade you to risk the planting and the waiting. Once the real thing arrives, you'll not be looking at the picture any more. You'll be burying your nose in the blossom and rejoicing at what has grown in the soil of your garden.

The Good News is that we no longer have to take the picture on the packet on trust. When the Guide appears, he not only shows us how our seeds can grow, but he reveals the fullness of that growth in himself. 'The human being, fully alive' is standing there, at the hinge of history – fulfilling, but also transcending the picture on the packet!

We hardly need to spell out the connections! We are seeds like that, but we don't really know anything about who we really are. And so we easily see ourselves, and each other, as a waste of space and throw ourselves away. Or we put the seed packet up on a little shrine, and worship it every so often, but never scatter the contents. God knows all about seeds like us. God plants them and waters them and waits for them to grow – as long as it takes. And we can either cooperate in the growth, or we can stay in the packet.

Which do *you* choose?

The story of the magic seed

Once upon a time there was a big family, who lived in a very poor country. Every year more children were born into this family, and every year they became poorer.

One day a traveller came through their country, offering packets of seed. 'Take my seeds,' he invited them, 'and go home and plant them in your poor soil, and soon you will have food growing in your garden, enough for all of you and to spare.'

Eagerly the family took the seed packet, and carried it home, and for years they talked about the traveller, and his great promise of a feast just there in their very own soil. Some of them said 'Let's do as the traveller said, and plant the seeds.' But others said, 'Oh *no*, these seeds are so very special, we must give them a place of honour in our home. It would be sacrilege to simply dig a hole and bury them. It would be a sin. It would be the height of folly.'

And so the careful ones won the day, and the seed packet was placed on the mantelpiece above the hearth, the most holy place that the family could find in its little hovel. Every day they venerated the picture on the packet, and prayed to their god that one day the promise of the traveller would be fulfilled. Generations were born and died, and the centuries passed by, and nothing happened. They stayed poor and they stayed hungry and the seed packet stayed above the hearth – high and dry!

Then one day there was a disaster. An earthquake shook the village, and the little hovel was destroyed. Flash floods swept through the fields where the family had lived. When the tumult subsided, there was almost no one left alive, and there was no sign of where the family had once lived out its days. But a few survivors remained, and among them a story was sometimes told – a half-remembered story, of how once a traveller had passed through, and made them a promise about a future beyond the horizon. They began to scan the distant skies, for glimpses of this future, but day after day the sun rose and the sun set and nothing changed.

One morning, two of these young people, who had been children when the earthquake came, sat in the devastated fields, gazing at the sun-rise, and wondering about the lost seeds.

'We need to search for that holy seed packet', one of them said. 'If we could only find it again, and venerate it as we used to do, all would be well.'

'I don't think we need to do that at all', replied the other. 'Just look at the field.'

And the field was springing green with fresh new growth, and at last the seed was free.

The lever of love

The human family has tried out all kinds of levers to shift the world into the place we want it to be. Some of them are very powerful. They can shape our lives and our choices, but do they make us more human?

Money is a prime mover. Global markets and multinational corporations wield enormous power over our hearts and minds, often in subtle and imperceptible ways. Money can buy military power, and the threat of force can bring most of us into line with the demands of a dominant regime. But does money make us more human?

A less aggressive, but equally insidious lever is the one that exploits the universal human desire to be liked, or, indeed, to be loved. This lever can tip us into spending more money than we can afford on merchandise marketed to make us look younger, slimmer, stronger, more masculine or feminine, and more desirable – but does it make us more human?

We are told that 'knowledge is power', and so in our generation, information has become a market commodity. To know enough about a person is to have control over them. To know enough about everyone is to have control over a society, a nation, a world. Our national and global databases can keep tabs on us all, but do they make us more human?

Status is another lever by which we may try to move the world around us. Celebrities are big news, and it appears that an amazingly high percentage of rational adults, well old enough to know better, actually follow and emulate the styles and idiosyncrasies of the personalities they see on their TV and cinema screens. If 'she' is wearing it today, 'we' will be buying it tomorrow. If 'he' drives it around Los Angeles, 'we' want to drive it in Slough. We may well spend more than we have to achieve our status, but does it make us more human?

These are just a few of the levers that motivate us, and persuade us do things that perhaps our deeper self would think twice about doing. So what lever does our Guide use?

Well, certainly none of the above. Jesus of Nazareth actively resisted the temptation to spread his message by using military force to challenge the hated occupying power. He taught that the poor should inherit the earth, those without status would be first in 'the Kingdom', and the marginalised ones – the ones whose faces didn't fit, the nameless, rootless, feckless ones, all those who fell off the rails were his special friends. Anyone who tried to pull rank with him got short shrift, but he always had time, and compassion, for the people that society would rather not know are there.

So what is this lever, that will move the world? At the start of this section, I suggested that it is the 'lever of love'. But what does that mean?

The word 'love' suffers, perhaps, from too good a press. It comes all gift-wrapped in pink ribbons and red hearts, and if we are not careful we will miss the point of it entirely. The most helpful thing I ever heard about love was this:

> Love is not an emotion. Love is a decision.

If we honestly want to know what love means, we really do need to strip it of its emotional baggage, down to its bones and its marrow. If it has any bones at all, they will be about the *decision* to relate to another in a loving, life-giving way, and not the *feelings* that may or may not accompany that decision.

I once went to Lourdes, the famous shrine in southern France. Actually, if I am honest, I tried to *avoid* Lourdes, while travelling back north from the Pyrenees, but the autoroute had other ideas, and in spite of myself, I was suddenly there. I had wanted to avoid it because I expected it to be commercialised and full of religious kitsch, and it was. But it also had love flowing through it like a river. I saw it in the eyes of the hundreds of people who had taken sick friends and relatives there, in hope that the journey might help them.

In countless faces I saw living evidence of the 'decision to love'. People who had given up their own chance of a holiday to tend the sick. Youngsters pushing the elderly and infirm in wheelchairs. Parents bringing up severely damaged children. I saw patience, and long-suffering, compassion, generosity, sacrifice, hope, trust … love! It seemed to me that the miracle of Lourdes lay less in the occasional stories of those who would return home physically cured, and more in the continuous stream of indomitable human loving that flowed through its streets and its holy places.

These were individual people who were making a decision for love – a decision to do the more human, the more loving, the more life-giving thing in the circumstances in which they found themselves. You don't need to go to Lourdes to see this kind of 'elected love'. You can see it wherever individuals are dedicated to putting the needs of others before their own immediate wishes.

Let us not forget, however, that our Guide urges us to love one another *as we love ourselves*. There is also a radical call to 'love ourselves', to give ourselves the esteem, the respect, the gentleness and consideration that the Guide himself gave to all those whose lives he touched, when he walked this earth two thousand years ago. Authentic self-respect leads to authentic respect for others and for all creation.

The earliest hominids began their growth into 'becoming human' when they became creatures who walked upright and used their hands to shape the world. It was a physical evolution.

Then followed the growth of the brain, and we evolved into creatures capable of rational thought, challenged to make choices about our actions. It was an evolution of the mind.

Now, perhaps, in the light of the fullness of life and humanity revealed in Jesus, now is the age of the Heart.

We have evolved physically to a high degree of sophistication. Our minds can grasp the workings of the universe, and our spirits can respond to the mystery in which we live and move and have our being. But our hearts – the key to making our choices under the guidance of love and wisdom – are surely still in their infancy.

The hinge of history opens into the innermost core of the human heart, where, if we follow our Guide, we will find ourselves, each other, the universe, and God.

What does 'love' mean for you? Are there any areas of your own life where you are living out of a decision to do the more loving thing, even though you may not have any loving feelings about it?

What do you think 'love' means for the human family as a whole?

Where do you find evidence of a growth in humanisation and a positive change of heart actually happening in our world today?

How might we nourish it? Where, in today's world, are the signs of 'the lever of love'?

The hinge of history swings on the lever of love. To be more specific, the transforming power of Jesus of Nazareth swings on your decisions in favour of the more loving choice and action. What might you change in your own living and choice-making to oil this hinge a little?

The heart has its own logic. The demands of love may turn our world upside-down and our souls inside-out. Are we ready for it ...?

To see the stars you may need to stand on your head ...

It could be tempting to imagine that our Guide is simply going to lead us into the future like some kind of Pied Piper of Hamelin, attracting us always further by the power of his own vision. This, however, would only be half of the truth. The other half is about the accumulation of all the self-focused choices humankind has been making for the past 100,000 years, or since the time when we first became rational creatures capable of choosing a course of action motivated solely by our own interest, or by the greater good of the whole of creation. It's about all those hard-wired connections in our brains that pre-program us for defence and attack.

Earlier in this book, we drew a parallel between the cumulative effects of these ego-centred choices and 'the bad branch' of 'the tree of the knowledge of good and evil'. Over the aeons of our evolution as *homo sapiens*, these effects have solidified into a rock-hard tendency in all of us to choose 'me first'. We do it as individuals. We do it collectively. It has limited but deadly effects in our interpersonal relationships. It has massive, global and destructive effects in our dealings with each other, nation to nation, race to race, gender to gender.

Even as the Guide leads us forward to the vision of life-in-all-its full-ness, he also reveals the overwhelming need to move beyond the instincts and compulsions of a mindset fixed on survival and domination. This is going to be no easy process. It isn't something we can possibly do for our-selves. Just as no child can learn to speak unless and until it is exposed to verbalisation by those who have mastered language, so do we have no chance at all of moving beyond the limitations and distortions that are the legacy of the earlier stages of 'becoming human' unless and until the Guide who is already fully evolved, fully alive, reveals the way, and empowers us to follow it.

The lever of love, if it is to be effective, isn't an attractive optional extra in the story of life, something we can activate as and when we feel like being loving. It is going to turn us on our heads.

The challenge to become fully human is going to be the most costly thing we ever embrace. It will demand a radical change of heart and mind, shifting our focus dramatically and irrevocably.

For example:

We tend to value ...	*But our Guide invites us to ...*
Achievement	Learn through our failures
Status	Learn the authentic humility of our interdependence
Acquisition	Let go of our attachment to created things
Security	Risk acknowledging our vulnerability
Certainty	Embrace the mystery of life
Control	Claim our freedom, and enable the freedom of others
Defensiveness, self-protection	Learn to trust each other and be worthy of trust ourselves
Dominion	Be willing to serve each other
Autonomy and individualism	Celebrate our interdependence
The accumulation of knowledge	Mature into wisdom
'Image'	Trust the deepest truth within our hearts and in each other
Supremacy and competition	Foster cooperation and mutuality
Pyramids of power	Form webs of relationship among equals
Fixed formulations of belief	Tell our stories and share our experience
'Either/or' solutions	Be open to 'both/and' possibilities

On the face of it, the qualities in the right-hand column sound easy. In practice they can prove incredibly difficult and the task that lies before us will be a lifelong challenge. The roots of most of the left-hand values go back to the savannah, and all the demands of survival in a hostile environment. They are the imprints of our lower brain, and the fruits of fear.

If you imagine it is going to be easy, just consider what we are saying, for example, when we campaign for a just solution to the challenge of third world poverty. If this is really to happen, then it means a great deal more than signing a cheque to our favourite charity or a petition to our governments. It is more likely to demand a drop of at least 40 per cent in our own standard of living in most of the western world. Imagine what this would mean for you personally, and you begin to have an idea of the cost of living true to the vision of Jesus of Nazareth.

Browse through the list of examples above, comparing our own tendencies with the values revealed by Jesus of Nazareth.
Which items in the list especially fire your imagination, and make you want to say 'Yes! I wish it could be like that.'
Which items irritate you, and leave you thinking 'No way! That's completely unrealistic.'
Does anything on the list leave you feeling threatened and defensive?
Now try to take a look at the roots of your reactions. What does this reveal about the most persistent roots of 'the old way' still lurking in your own mind and heart?

But let us not despair, because there is real evidence of the effects of the lever of love already in our world.

For the first time, humankind is beginning to realise the positive power that can be generated when large numbers of people come together with a common focus on bringing about change for the better for the sake of all creation. To everyone's amazement, such a concentration of peaceful 'people power' in 1989 broke the stranglehold of totalitarianism in one Eastern European country after another. A few years later the power of world public opinion and the resilience and determination of people of conscience, black and white, in South Africa, brought an end to apartheid in that country.

At the turn of the millennium, we had the opportunity to celebrate this threshold as a world family. Through global television, for the first time we could all share in everyone's celebrations. As the dawn of the new millennium swept around the globe, from time zone to time zone, we rejoiced, we sang, we danced, we meditated, and one universal call was heard from nation after nation: the call for peace – the deep peace which is so much more than the absence of conflict – the peace that the world cannot give, and which all our hearts long for.

Events such as the *Live Aid* and *Live 8* concerts focus this human longing and positive energy, and so do peaceful mass demonstrations expressing the overwhelming human desire for non-violent solutions to the world's problems. Mass expressions of solidarity and support are evidence of the lever of love, when thousands of strangers gather together in a spirit of genuine community in the face of some disaster or loss. In Britain we witnessed this, for example, after the school massacre at Dunblane, on the death of the very vulnerable and much-loved Princess Diana, after the London bombings in July 2005 and in the many times we have paused, as a people, to mark our sorrow and compassion in minutes of silence together. Such spontaneous gatherings are now common all over the world. They are one of the signs of our times, and they are also signs of the lever of love in operation.

Many people are also discovering the deep well of spiritual power to be found in stillness, in silent reflection, in meditation, and in authentic communion with God, with themselves, with others and with the created world.

All around the world, literally millions of ordinary human beings, both individually and collectively, are saying, in so many different ways: 'There has to be a better way, and we are capable, together, of finding it and making it happen.' This is a decision that we are making together – a decision for love.

All things considered, are we moving forwards or slipping back, as a human family on the quest to become more fully human?
What do you think?

Two cocktails

If you recall our earlier excursion into the beginnings of our species on earth, and the transition from Neanderthal Man to the beginnings of modern *homo sapiens*, you may remember that anthropologists and palaeontologists have noticed that for a long time there was no real development in how we lived, how we hunted, how we made and used our primitive tools. In fact, there was no evidence of the use of imagination, or the exercise of any creativity. Until that great leap forward, when our early ancestors began to ask questions like: 'What if we were to try this … ?'

The little phrase 'what if' speaks volumes. It reveals a sense of the future. 'We have, so far, always done this, but perhaps in the future we might try …' This imaginative leap forward seems to have begun when our brains evolved into the higher model with its *cortex*. The enhanced model of the brain was capable of processing reflective and deductive thought, posing questions to itself and implementing its answers. It was the beginning of *imagination*.

But, as we have seen, a sense of the future can bear both creative and destructive fruits. As with every other development through which we have passed, the tree of the new knowledge has two branches. One of these branches bears fruits that we could call the fruits of *fear*, for example:

- What if the tribe across the valley is planning to attack us? We need to take pre-emptive action.
- What if my companions are trying to deceive me? I need to be suspicious and defensive.
- What if the other members of the tribe don't want to do things my way? How can I dominate or intimidate them into doing so?
- What if I can't win the mate that I desire? How might I get my way by force?
- What if the food runs out? Maybe I can steal some from my neighbour, or take his land from him.

The other branch bears fruits that spring from *love*. For example:

- What if we could teach our children more effectively? Let's find ways to educate them.

- What if our companions fall sick? Let's look for new ways to heal them.
- What if there is another land beyond this ocean. Let's go and explore.
- What if that is a human settlement on the horizon? Let's seek friendship with them.
- What if we could harness the power of the animals? Let's try to work cooperatively with them.

Gerard W. Hughes, author of the best-selling book *God of Surprises*, warns us that 'fear and imagination are a lethal cocktail'. Few of us would doubt this. Which of us has not gone down the spiral of fearing something in the future, and then (usually in the darkest hours of the night) imagining worse and worse possible scenarios of what we fear. The result is a rapid and deadly descent to the basement of our minds where our worst demons wait to entangle us in our accelerating terrors.

But if fear and imagination together form such a deadly brew, what kind of cocktail might we expect if we mix *love* and imagination?

If you would like a taster of these two cocktails, just ponder the two lists of 'fruits' above. In the second part of each proposition you can see how the cocktail is shaping up.

When the cocktail is a mix of fear and imagination, the result is destructive. Imagination is being used to make something neutral into something potentially deadly, and fear feeds upon fear.

When the cocktail is a mix of love and imagination, the result is that something new comes to birth that has the potential to benefit all the human family. When love and imagination meet there is no limit to what can happen, and how far the vision can lead.

I suggest that it is precisely the cocktail of love and imagination that Jesus of Nazareth mixes for us. He invites us, again and again, to look at how things *are* around us, and then to imagine how things *could be*, if we could dare to use the lever of love.

It begins with the way he tells stories and makes connections: 'Imagine your friend has a splinter in his eye. You want to help get it out, but there is a whole branch in your own eye. Wouldn't it be better to put your own house in order before you try to sort out your friend? This is what it means to withhold your judgement about other people.'

And it goes on to pervade his teaching on how a better, a more truly human community might work:

'Your old mindset says, "Take revenge – an eye for an eye." But what if there were a better way, a way based on love and growth and a willingness to forgive and to learn from our mistakes?'

'Your old mindset says, "Make sure you keep all the rules and stay on the right side of God." But what if there were a better way, not based on fear of losing God's favour, but on your own heart's desire to live "God's dream"?'

In the next leg of our journey we will go on to explore this new way in more depth.

However, there is a big problem. The lever of love can make serious enemies among those who gain and hold their power by instilling fear into others. Where light shines, there will be a shadow. The more pure and clear the light, the darker the shadow.

What happens when our Guide, the one who is fully human, fully alive, and fully at one with God, collides with the powers of darkness that subtly and silently distort the hidden depths of our hearts?

Is the cocktail of love and imagination strong enough to draw us beyond the influence of these instincts of survival, fear and domination that are the hallmarks of our primitive (lower brain) 'me first' mentality?

When push comes to shove, which cocktail will win the day?

Have you swallowed the cocktail of fear and imagination lately? How did it feel? Have you tasted the cocktail of love and imagination? If so, what were the circumstances?
Dare you let it intoxicate you?

A narrow way

There is a rock in Cumbria, in England's Lake District, called Nape's Needle. At the summit of this rock is a narrow gap and the challenge to climbers is to scale the rock (no easy feat in itself) and then to pass physically through the gap and descend the rock on the other side. This is called 'threading the needle'. You can only do it if you are slim, and, most crucially, if you have no backpack with you, or any other encumbrances. There is only space there for a single human being to pass through, with absolutely no extras.

Jesus sometimes spoke of 'a narrow way', that many would seek and few would find. The fullness of life, he taught, is found, ironically, in letting things go, not in accumulating more of them. This, of course, flies right in the face of almost everything our own consumer society proposes to us as 'the good life'. To take on board this wisdom is to make a real act of faith. It demands that we trust that this 'letting go' is truly the way to grow into the fullness of our being. Why would anyone (programmed as we are to obey the promptings of our lower brain with all its fear/greed agenda) entrust their few short years on earth to such a vision?

Jesus surely knew these doubts, and he addresses them in fresh and imaginative ways, as we shall explore in the next section. But the main thing he does is to live out, in his own flesh and blood, the walking of the narrow way, right into the point where it appears to disintegrate into nothing at all, where he comes up against a clear 'No further!' sign, and where the light of his own life is definitively extinguished.

What can we say about how the light indeed once shone in our midst and we put it out? And what can we say about the lights of hope, of trust, of love that once leapt up in our own hearts, perhaps when we were young and still untouched by disappointment and regret, and how now they have turned to ash? ... because the two are connected! Jesus of Nazareth emerged from among us as the one whose life is totally at one with the source of all life. Yet after a few short years of living and teaching the new way that would take the human family beyond where we are, to all that we can become, he was executed as a common criminal, and buried in a stranger's grave.

The eye of the needle doesn't get much narrower than this. And yet Jesus of Nazareth did 'thread the needle'. Unencumbered by any baggage, and stripped down to the naked core of his being, the pure essence of himself, he passed through the narrow path, and opens up the same possibility for all who dare to follow him.

The death of Jesus, and even more, his resurrection, confront us with many unresolved questions, perhaps the most difficult ones being:
   Why did Jesus actually have to die?
   Did Jesus really 'rise' from death, and if so, what does this mean for us?

Many of us have, of course, been given the 'right answers' to these questions since early childhood. Others have grown up in 'unknowing'. Either way, if we are to let go of *everything*, to pass along the narrow path, we may need to go beyond the inherent limitations of these 'received certainties', and discover for ourselves what these questions really mean for us.

Why did Jesus have to die? Was it a necessary blood sacrifice demanded by a vengeful God, to pay the price and take the punishment for the 'fall from grace' of humankind? This suggestion poses more questions than it provides answers. What kind of 'God' is this, who will not be satisfied until he has his pound of flesh and dispenses justice by means of the ultimate death penalty (a form of punishment that most civilised peoples today have rejected as unworthy of humanity)? What kind of disobedience is being atoned for? Why did it all have to wait until two thousand years ago, if the 'original sin' goes back at least 100,000 years?

There are other ways of understanding Jesus' death. We have already noticed that when a bright, clear light shines out, it casts a deep dark shadow. This fact of physics is also a fact of human nature. One who lives completely true to everything it means to be a fully evolved and complete and perfect human being will inevitably provoke all the shadow side of our still very immature and incomplete human nature. From where we are presently standing on the line of evolution, we cannot even imagine how sharp this provocation will be, and how deadly. When pure love encounters deep fear, the fear will rise up and seek to overcome the love, which threatens its power base. We see glimpses of this dynamic at work when, for example, youthful idealism is crushed by sardonic cynicism, and the simplicity of altruistic love is demeaned by those who search for hidden selfish motivations.

When the fully human life emerges on planet Earth in the person of Jesus of Nazareth, the shadow it provokes is immense – big enough to have life put to death – apparently ... ! And for anyone who follows down this narrow path of trust and faith that life is stronger than anything that can be ranged against it, there will be a personal 'eye of the needle', which Jesus expressed in his warning 'You too will get crucified in your own way, if you try to live life by the vision I will give you. But trust me, and follow me anyway, and I will show you that you will not only come through the narrow path, but it will lead you to a fullness of life beyond anything you can imagine.'

The only way Jesus could possibly convince us of the truth of this promise is to model the way for us – not just by living it, but by dying it, and, indeed, passing beyond it.

So, did he rise from death? And if so, what does this mean?

In my own mind, and my own heart, there is actually no doubt that Jesus of Nazareth, the human person who lived fully true to what it means to be human, moved beyond death to become the Christ, a presence who now transcends time and space, and is in the eternal now, for ever at one with the source and the destiny of life. How this happened, in physical and metaphysical terms is Mystery, and I am pre-pared to allow it to be so, knowing that my mind is far too under-evolved to fathom its depths.

However, we do know, from twenty-first century physics, that energy and matter are interchangeable, and that all that is may manifest itself in form of particles or waves – particles of 'matter' (for example the particles that form a human person who can be identified and related to) or waves of energy with no permanent physical position. I find no difficulty in believing that Jesus of Nazareth consciously reached this point of transcendence, and continues to be present to receptive hearts and minds, always drawing us, too, towards our own transcendence.

In the mystery of resurrection, Jesus transcends the historic person, the unique configuration of particles, and becomes a wave of pure energy – the energy of Love itself – the energy that many call the Holy Spirit. The historic person of Jesus becomes the Christ, the anointed one, the one who is completely at one with the source of all being, and calls all who have ears to hear and hearts to respond, to grow in and through that Spirit into the same fullness of life.

If this were just a statement of my acceptance, at the rational level, of a proposition of faith, then it would not be worth the paper I am writing it on. I offer it to you because I don't just *believe* it – I *know* it from my own experience, and in the form of heart-knowledge. I know, from my own struggles along the narrow way, that the presence of a transcendent mystery is a fact and the touch of God is real, and is effective.

How can I be so sure? Perhaps this 'touch of God' can only be expressed in the language of prayer …

When each raw skin has been peeled away from my well-defended life, you have made sense of it, promising me that with each stripping, we come closer to the heart of the matter.

When my life has felt fragmented and pointless, you have shown me that 'atonement' is actually about 'at-one-ment', and that my own fractured parts are there in that One-ness, even if I can't yet see that for myself.

When I have been close to despair, someone has crossed my path, spoken a word, offered a gesture of love and encouragement, given me a reason to make the next few steps, and left me knowing, for sure, that such people come in your spirit, whether they know it or not.

When I have wept in the darkness, or fallen into an exhausted sleep, you have sometimes touched my dreams. When I have struggled to resolve a problem, and then given up in frustration, the solution has sometimes presented itself unexpectedly in a moment of absolute clarity, and we have moved on, together.

You haven't worked the miracles I asked for, but you have shown me what your shalom-peace can be like – only occasionally, but to have known that perfect peace just once, is to know that it is always there, just as the sun is always there even though clouds veil its light most of the time.

You haven't let me get away with worshipping you from afar, or putting you into a religious box, but have challenged me to walk with you, moment by moment, along the particular narrow way that my own life leads me into. You have gently persuaded me to set aside everything that would stop us 'threading the needle', even though, when we got down to the heart of it, some of what I needed to shed turned out to be aspects of religion itself.

You have made your ever-presence real for me, palpable, and effective, in ways my heart never could deny, and my deepest desire is to let that presence guide me, and all creation, to the fullness of life that your life reveals and enables.

Why did Jesus have to die? And did he really rise?
What do you think? What does this mystery mean to you?
What does your experience suggest?
Listen to your heart as well as to your mind.

The portage pine

In spite of seven years of school French, when I first came across the word 'portage', on a lakeside in the wilds of northern Ontario, I had no idea what it might mean. I checked the map, and found it engraved there too, mysteriously, at strategic points at the end of various lakes.

Life is the best teacher, we are told, and it was life that eventually taught me the meaning of 'portage'. We were out on the lake, in a little canoe, and exhibiting more enthusiasm than expertise. By the grace of God and a following wind, we found ourselves at the end of the lake, having arrived there without submersion, and then what?

It is said that if you know how, you can get by water from Ontario right across the vast continent of Canada, to Alberta. Our problem was simply to get from the end of one lake to the beginning of the next. Even though this part of Canada is one huge network of lakes and rivers, if you are in the middle of a lake, surrounded by dense forest, there is no possible way of guessing where you should head for, to find the path that leads you to the next lake. The sign 'portage', either on the map or on the lakeside itself, tells you:

'If you head for here, you will find the beginning of the narrow path that will lead you to the next lake, the next stage of your voyage. At this point you will have to carry your canoe along a narrow path, until you reach the beginning of the next stage of your journey.'

This unexpected sign delighted me for more reasons than the obvious one. The more I thought about it, the more it reminded me of the vision of Jesus of Nazareth. We, who are solidly settled in the lake called *homo sapiens*, and probably thinking this is all there is, have no idea where our human story might go next, or, indeed, whether there really is anything beyond where we are now. Jesus, the fully evolved, fully alive human person shows us where the narrow way to the next stage of our journey begins. He does more than this. He walks the narrow way along with us, lives it and dies it with us, until we break through to the 'lake' of a new life that currently lies way beyond our sight.

Very struck with this connection, I was later telling some friends about my discovery, and one of them asked me whether I knew how the first people to sail their canoes along these lakes had been able to find the portage point to get to the next lake. Needless to say, I had no idea, and he went on to explain.

The first peoples to sail these lakes were the First Nations peoples, and they would have found the best crossing points to the next lake by trial and error. Once the best route had been discovered, they would have wanted to give a signal to all those who would come after them. There were no maps then, and no painted wooden signposts. They solved the problem by seeking out the tallest pine tree close to the start of the transit path. They would then strip away all the branches from this tree, leaving only the 'tassle' – the little cluster of branches right at the top of the tree. As a result, all the strength of the chosen tree would go into its upward growth, and so it would rise even further above the general height of the surrounding pines, and it would also be easily recognised by its distinctive 'tassle'. People in canoes would see it a long way ahead, and know where to head for, to reach the best transit path to the next lake along their journey.

When I think of Jesus, especially in his final days on earth, I see him as a kind of Portage Pine. He too was stripped, not only physically, but in every way, before being sent to his terrible death. He too stood out above all other human beings by a long way, and even wore the 'tassle' – a crown of thorns. His life, death and resurrection announce to all of us:

> *'This is where the narrow path begins, that will lead you to the next stage of your great adventure in "becoming human". Trust me, and follow me, even though the path is so narrow and the way may be uncomfortable or even dangerous. Follow me, and trust me for all that lies ahead. I am walking with you all the way.'*

When you reach the portage point you have to hoist your canoe, upside-down, onto your back, and carry it along the path until you reach the next expanse of water. It isn't an easy undertaking, but it's the only way, if you are serious about journeying on.

Now that we, the human family, have reached the portage point in the story of our ongoing evolution, our lives will be turned upside down like that canoe. All the non-essentials will fall out, and have to be left behind. When we step onto the narrow path, there is only room enough for ourselves, our lives, and our guide.

Yet here too, recalling the Laetoli footprints that declared us to be bipedal three million years ago, we again find three sets of footprints – those of a young couple fleeing with their child from an outbreak of 'ethnic cleansing' in the Middle East two thousand years ago. But this time, the prints of the *child* lead the way …

Are you ready for the next lake?

FLYING LESSONS

'She followed slowly and she needed time,
as though some long ascent were not yet by;
and yet: as though, when she had ceased to climb,
she would no longer merely walk, but fly.'

Rainer Maria Rilke 'Going Blind'
Translated by J. B. Leishman

Pilgrims on the path

There are no five-star hotels on the narrow transit path that leads to the next lake. There are no cathedrals, no city halls, no rallying grounds, no corporate headquarters. It's a *very* narrow path. You go along it in single file. Everyone has to make his or her own way.

But that doesn't mean travelling in isolation. Because there are tents and resting places. And there are little camping spots, and clearings in the forest where two or more can gather with the guide and share the journey. In fact the Guide makes two important promises to everyone who sets out along the transit path:

To each individual pilgrim he says: 'I am with you all the way.'

And to all who embark on the journey he says: 'Whenever and wherever two or more of you stop for a while to reflect on where you are, and where I am, I will be right there among you.'

And there are no clocks and timetables, and no one is standing along the route to measure who is 'winning', because every path is unique. There are no 'winners'. But far more important than this: *there are no losers!*

There is no hierarchy or pecking order along the way. Just travellers like ourselves, all journeying in trust, because no one actually knows what the next lake is like, whatever they may tell you! There is no list of rules, but just one simple instruction: 'Love and respect every other traveller, and be kind to yourself.'

There is no definitive map. That may shock and dismay you, but there is something better than a map to follow. There is a dream. A big dream that embraces all our little dreams. It is a dream we follow, and the dream leaves its traces everywhere along the path, for those who have eyes to see.

How do you follow a dream?

By noticing those traces.

By looking out for the footprints the Guide has left.

By meeting some of the people who have followed the dream before you.

By sharing your experience with others who are also walking the way along with you.

During this part of our journey, we will make a little pilgrimage ourselves. We'll meet a few of the people on the way. We'll listen to their stories, about themselves, and about their encounters with the Guide, who is also the dreamer, and perhaps they'll listen to ours.

Like the subject of the words by Rilke, we 'follow slowly' and we need time — aeons of it — to walk the narrow way to transcendence. Can we trust that we too, having walked so far, shall fly?

But to follow a trail you need to be able to recognise what you are looking for — the hints and glimpses that what you are seeking has passed this way. So before we set out to journey as pilgrims along the transit path, let's just pause for a moment to look at the shape of our own footprint, and at the footprint of our Guide ...

How much does your footprint weigh?

According to Paul Kennedy of Yale University, writing in the *Observer* of the population of the United States:

'We comprise slightly less than 5 per cent of the world's population, but we imbibe 27 per cent of the world's annual oil production, create and consume nearly 30 per cent of its Gross World Product, and – get this – spend a full 40 per cent of *all* the world's defence expenditure. By my calculation, the Pentagon's budget is nowadays roughly equal to the defence expenditure of the next nine or ten highest defence-spending nations - which has never before happened in history. That is indeed a heavy footprint. How do we explain it to others - and to ourselves?'

A heavy footprint indeed, and those of us who are not citizens of the United States have no reason to feel absolved. If we live anywhere in the (so-called) 'developed' world our footprint will not be much lighter!

Nor does our footprint stop at simply the amount of the world's resources we use per head of population. It is made heavier by the stamp of our whole way of life and our determination to impose it on the rest of the world and its peoples. Any nations, institutions or individuals who exercise political, economic, or cultural power over others potentially impoverish and enslave billions of men, women and children, and have absolutely nothing to congratulate themselves about.

It doesn't have to be like that.

On Good Friday morning one year I watched a spellbinding programme on television. It was presented by John Bell of the Iona Community, a well-known and much-loved musician and worker for justice, peace and for the Christian vision at its best. John was filming in South Africa, and drawing connections between South Africa's turbulent history and the events of Good Friday two thousand years ago in Jerusalem. He was inviting viewers to recognise that the persecution and the crucifixion of what is good and true in humanity still goes on, undiminished.

During the programme, John invited a black South African woman to share something of her story. She was running an orphanage for children whose parents had died of HIV/AIDS. Her love and commitment to these children was total and unconditional. Her words were simple and direct.

'What would you like to leave behind as your legacy when you die?'
John asked her.

She thought about the question for a few moments. Her answer took
me by surprise:

'When I die,' she said, 'I hope I will have spent everything I have.'

Another brief pause, and she added:

'When I meet my maker, I want to be empty-handed, because I want
to have used up completely every gift God has given me. When I die I
want to leave nothing behind, except a little footprint, that might help
others find their way.'

What a light and slender footprint that would be.

Jesus left no obvious or permanent 'prints' behind. He wrote no books,
achieved no academic status, created nothing of artistic value. He left us
neither a philosophy nor a theology. He established no new form of
earthly government, and there are many who would say he established no
new religion, no church, no organisation, no hierarchy and no institution
.

When he died he had spent everything he had, and he returned into
the eternal now having used up completely every gift that God had given
him. Leaving only his spirit, and a slender pointer in the direction of life,
he entrusted the ongoing evolution of the human family to a few men
and women who had understood who he was and were willing to set out
along the narrow path that leads to the future.

To follow his dream is to be awake and alive to the slightest stirrings
of his living spirit, not to seek for mere monuments of his life on earth.
To follow the dream is to tread lightly upon the earth, so lightly that we
can almost fly.

How much does *your* footprint weigh?

Could it really be, as Jesus suggests, that we are rich only in what we
give away, secure only in what we relinquish, great only in our littleness
and strong only in our vulnerability?

This paradox, this upturning of all our assumptions and expectations,
is the hallmark of the narrow way that leads us to all it means to be fully
human. It points us towards the seed of divinity sleeping in the ground of
our being, and shows us how to bring that seed to life.

Let's spend a while now following the narrow trail that leads to the future.
Let's be alert to the signs of the Guide's prints along the way, learning to
notice when we are following *his* prints, and when our own, much
heavier, footprints are drawing us perhaps in other directions than the
best. And let's see who we meet along the way, and what they have to tell
us …

The cook's tale

I'm a practical person. Dreams have never been my thing. Who would ever go off on a journey into the unknown, following just a dream?!

Setting out on this path was completely out of character for me. I really don't know what possessed me, and every morning as I journey on, I still wonder whether I did the right thing. I wonder … and yet, I *know*.

It began a long way back. In those days we lived a quiet life, my sister and myself – our parents were long dead, and neither of us had ever married. We lived in a cottage in a small village called Bethany, not a million miles from Jerusalem, but far enough away to avoid all the big-town bustle and noise.

It might have been because we lived such a quiet life that Jesus often came to us when he was needing a bolt-hole to escape the 'madding crowds'.

But as I come to think about it, there is something laughable in saying I lived in a quiet spot to avoid the bustle of the city … because actually, I realise now, I created my *own* bustle and noise. I was always a 'do-er.' If I wasn't busy, if I wasn't 'gainfully employed', I felt guilty. Know the feeling?

One evening Jesus dropped in unexpectedly. He was exhausted, and he just wanted a space to be. But I – of course! – immediately went into overdrive. What could we eat? Hospitality is a big 'must' for us. To feed the guest is a number one priority. But here I go again, trying to justify myself and my existence.

So I bustled around in the kitchen, scraping carrots, scrubbing potatoes, chopping meat and onions, and working out at the back of my mind what wine I should offer, and whether there was time to bake fresh bread. Busy, busy, busy, and … well, actually I was getting more and more frazzled and frustrated. Why is it always me that gets to do the work? And my thoughts roamed through the house to where Jesus and my sister Mary were sitting together, just talking, and listening. Jesus was talking dream-talk. He has a dream. It's a God-dream, he says, and it will lead us to beyond anything we could ever imagine for ourselves, just as a seed dreams secretly of the flower it will one day be, even though it has never seen a flower.

And me – I get to feed the dreamer.

Well, I had had enough of dreaming for the day, and if I am honest I was angry with myself. If I was missing out on something, whose fault was it, I wondered. I didn't like the answer I discovered. I didn't like to think it might be down to me and my own choices. So I blamed it all on my sister Mary. I stomped into the room where they were sitting, and blasted off at Jesus:

'I'm in the kitchen all alone, trying to get us a meal. Can't you tell Mary to get herself moving for a change, and give me a hand?'

Oh, I can tell you, I regretted my words the minute they were out. I sounded like a petulant schoolgirl. I could hear that myself, but I couldn't take back the words I had spoken. I wanted to sink into the floor. I glared at Mary in my fury. I didn't dare meet Jesus' eyes.

I don't know how long I would have stood there in the doorway, stuck halfway between rage and shame. But I felt an arm around my shoulder, and the gentle pressure of Jesus' hand drawing me closer to where the two of them were sitting.

'Martha, Martha', he said. 'You are always so busy, and believe me I deeply appreciate the way you make me so welcome here and feed me so well. But how about if *I* feed *you* for a change? The cook is starving, isn't she?'

That was too much. The tears started to prickle in my eyes, but he just drew me closer. The three of us sat down together. He kept hold of my hand. I guess he noticed it was trembling.

For a while nobody said anything at all. We just sat there in a deep, companionable silence. I felt myself coming to rest again. If you can imagine a glass of muddy water, all stirred up and murky, and then watch as it settles and gradually becomes crystal clear, that was how I felt. When the water was settled, and we were all three at peace, Jesus told us something about his dream that I will never forget.

'My friends, it's good to care for others. Some people spend their whole lives caring for others. So much so that they never come to rest themselves. But have you ever thought where the energy for all that caring comes from? Have you ever tried to cook a meal without fire? Or to do the washing without any water?

This is why I come here. I want to care for God's people, but I can't do anything at all without the energy of God's love and God's spirit flowing in and through me. And where do I find that deep source of energy that I need? I find it in stillness. And I find it in the quiet love that flows to me from other people.

One of the places I find that stillness and that love is here with the two of you. I need that even more than I need food, and I need both of you to be part of it. I want you to discover for yourselves the deep well of stillness within you, and to know that you can draw from this well whenever you are weary or anxious. Nothing else will ever satisfy the thirst and hunger in your hearts.'

Since then things have changed. Mary and I share the dream together now, and we even share the chores, but we have learned to live much more simply, since we set off along this path.

The cook is well fed now, and that makes me an even better cook. And the recipe lies in the stillness, where there is time and space just to 'be'.

★ ★ ★

In our world today, 'busy-ness' is valued and stillness is often despised. Even our holidays can become 'activity holidays', from which we return even more stressed than when we began.

The Guide says the key to the dream lies in stillness, not in frantic activity. He tells us there is no need to justify our existence in the world. There is nothing to prove. Just hear those words, *really* hear them: '*There is nothing to prove*'!

He invites us to take quality time just to be still, to listen to his suggestions, to tell him how we are feeling, to reflect on the journey.

What about you?

Is your inner 'cook' starving?

Where does stillness figure in your life?
Are you satisfied that there is enough of it?
If not, can you do anything to create a bit more oasis time for yourself?

There is a Martha and a Mary inside all of us.
How do you feel about your own 'Martha' and 'Mary'?
Which of them do you give more attention to?
Do you value one of them more highly than the other?
Is it time perhaps to look again at the balance between them?

The critic's tale

It started off as a typical working day. The crowing of the cockerel from the farm down the road woke me up. I went to the window, had a good stretch and took a deep breath of fresh morning air, and looked out.

Well, I'd been keeping a watchful eye on the goings-on across the road for quite a while. She's up to no good, that young woman. Not long married, and her husband working away. Who knows what she's up to? Not that it's any business of mine, of course, but we all have a responsibility to do what we can to keep up the standards. One rotten apple, and soon the whole crate starts to go off …

Anyway, that morning my suspicions were confirmed. As I stood there behind the curtains, I saw her door open, and I watched, aghast, as this young man slunk off down the street. Now what, I ask you, is a young man like him doing sneaking out of a young married woman's house at that hour in the morning?

I wasted no more time. Calling a few equally upright friends, I went over there straight away, and together we hauled her out onto the street, just as she was, in her flimsy nightdress. We didn't stop to ask questions. We dragged her, kicking and screaming, to the court, and delivered her to the official guardians of morality. We all knew what would happen. She would be stoned to death. Our law demanded it.

But it wasn't going to be quite that simple. By now quite a crowd was gathering to see what all the commotion was about. The religious authorities were there in the Temple all right, but so was this other fellow. This Jesus.

Why they didn't just get on with the job themselves, instead of involving him, I'll never know. They had already decided to have her stoned, but for no apparent reason, they dragged her over to where Jesus was sitting, and put the question to him. 'This woman has been caught in the very act of adultery. Our law says she must be stoned to death. What do *you* say?'

Well, what *did* he say? Nothing at all! What kind of an answer is that? For what seemed like ages, he just sat there, doodling with a stick in the sand. Everyone held their breath. Whatever was coming? The *woman* (I'll not do her the honour of giving her a name!) cringed on the floor – as well she might. Some people were already choosing their stones to hurl at her. There wasn't a stone big enough for my satisfaction! People like her need flogging off the face of the earth.

I almost missed the moment when he finally looked up, and gazed at all of us. 'I suggest that those among you who have never done anything wrong, never made a mistake, should be the first to throw their stones,' he calmly announced.

The woman braced herself for the impact. Jesus continued to gaze at us, as though the woman had done nothing. Why did I get the feeling that it was *us* who were under scrutiny and not her? Why, in particular, did I get the feeling that his piercing gaze was boring a hole right through *me*?

One by one folk began to leave. Stones were dropped and left behind. Soon there was no one left except her, and him, and me.

He turned to her first: 'Has anyone condemned you?' he asked. 'No sir.' 'Neither do I. Go home, and think about how you really want your life to be.'

She left. And I wanted to leave too. But he hadn't finished.

'If you have a minute, I'd like to tell you a story,' he said. I looked at him hard and long. What was he up to? What were his motives? Was he trying to make a fool of me? But his face was relaxed, and his eyes were kind. In spite of myself, I moved a little closer to him.

'Have a seat,' he invited me.

I sat down beside him. 'Just imagine,' he began, 'that it is your birthday. Two friends send you a gift. One of these gifts is wrapped in a beautiful gilded box, and tied with ribbons. But when you open it you find, to your disgust, that it contains only rotten fruit. The other gift is delivered in a torn, dirty box, already green with mould. You hardly like to touch this box, but when you finally open it up, inside it you find a beautiful rose. Which gift would you value more?'

'The rose', I replied, somehow feeing that I had walked into a trap.

He was silent for a while. Then he continued. 'The woman you wanted to stone to death has a rose in her heart', he said. 'But to see it you have to look deeper than the outside wrapping. You have to look with the eyes of the heart.'

I wanted to leave him. I was feeling distinctly uncomfortable, but he took my arm and looked straight into my eyes.

'There's a rose inside you too,' he said, and there was love in his eyes. 'Let me show you how to find it.'

So here I am, a pilgrim on this path, looking for my rose. I'm still not so sure there is really a rose in me. Maybe I've never really believed that. Maybe that's why I find it so hard to see the good in others. But I am finding that I see a lot more roses than stones now along my way, and I'm much more careful now before I throw a box away!

* * *

Mr or Mrs Critic is still with us. Still *in* us, even! One afternoon when I was in our local town, I caught sight of a girl of about fourteen, wearing the uniform of the school my daughter attended. I recognized her. She had a reputation. She was known as a trouble-maker, a bit of a rebel, a teachers' nightmare. It wasn't too difficult to make further assumptions about her. Maybe she was doing drugs. Probably she was promiscuous. Most likely she wouldn't do well in her exams. She was clearly from a bad home. She was headed nowhere …

I watched her walking through the gardens at the centre of the town's underpass system. Her skirt was round her waist. Her eyes were heavy. Her gait was defiant. But her gaze was fixed on a beggar who was always down there, with his collecting tin and his wretched expression. She obviously knew him. She stopped to say hello to him. They chatted for a while, and then she went off to the nearby fast food takeaway, and brought him something to eat. They parted like a pair of old friends.

I saw that girl through different eyes that afternoon. And suddenly the gardens down there were bright with roses.

Think of those people who most irritate you.
Jesus would see the rose inside them.
Can you?
Can you believe in the rose inside yourself?

The undesirable alien's tale

Borders are a terrible thing. Nothing separates people like borders, and labels. I should know. I lived all my life on a border, between Judaea and Samaria. We were the hated neighbours. In fact we weren't regarded as 'neighbours' at all, but as the lowest form of life. The Jews wouldn't touch us – literally. They wouldn't eat out of a plate we had used or drink from a cup that our hands had touched. And the distrust was mutual. It was serious apartheid.

One day I had to make a journey, from Jerusalem to Jericho. Nobody in their right mind goes that way if they don't have to. The terrain is wild and desolate, an ideal hiding place for thugs and muggers, and worse. But I had no choice, so I saddled up the mule, and off we went.

I got to the steep bit, where the road drops sharply. There you don't just have to look out for thieves, but you are very likely to take a fall as well, if your animal stumbles on the steep gradient. I was moving very carefully and slowly. Maybe that's why I was so aware of what was going on ahead of me. There was a man lying in the track, obviously injured.

I wasn't alone on the road that day. There were two other riders ahead of me. From the distance I thought I could see that one was dressed as a priest. A little way behind him rode a Levite, someone who serves in the temple too, but is a bit lower in the pecking order. Neither of them would have had a good word to say to me, so I kept my distance. I certainly didn't figure anywhere at all in the pecking-order.

The first of them reached the place where the injured man was lying. I couldn't believe it. He rode round him, making sure to make no physical contact or even to let his mule touch him. So much for ritual purity I thought. But would the second do the same? And sure enough, he skirted round the man too, with his head turned very deliberately in the opposite direction. What I don't see doesn't concern me, sort of thing.

Well, I am neither pure nor clean, at least not in their eyes. I did what anyone (well, almost anyone) would have done. I gave the guy first aid as best I could, then hoisted him onto my mule and took him to the nearest village and settled him in an inn there. Thank God, he recovered from his injuries. When I came back that way a few days later, and turned into the inn to settle the bill, he was all smiles and thank yous. I wasn't looking for gratitude. I was just glad to see him on his feet again.

In a funny kind of way I felt sorry for those two who were travelling ahead of me. It must be pretty difficult to live with such a convoluted set of rules like they do, when it means choosing between keeping the rules and doing the decent thing as a human being. What is 'human' anyway, I sometimes wonder.

The whole episode had an unexpected sequel. Not long afterwards my travels brought me once again into contact with the Jews who hate us so much. There was a crowd gathered round an itinerant preacher. Out of curiosity I stopped to listen, and then I rather wished I hadn't. It's a weird feeling when you find yourself listening to your own story.

The news of the injured man had travelled further than I had! Maybe the innkeeper spread the word, but here was this guy talking about the incident, and I couldn't help but recognise the circumstances again. The preacher was a Jew – no doubt about that. But here he was telling the crowd how a Samaritan, of all people, had done the right thing on the road to Jericho, while a priest and a Levite had passed by, leaving the casualty lying in a pool of blood. There he stood, actually giving credit to a Samaritan, and holding me up as an example. That has to be a first!

I slipped away. It was embarrassing!

But I didn't get far. Shortly afterwards I heard footsteps behind me and when I turned round, half expecting another ambush, since I was an undesirable alien in this part of the world, who should be there but the itinerant preacher himself.

'Mind if I walk with you a while?' he asked, loudly so that anyone around us could easily hear. 'Sure,' I replied. 'It would be a pleasure.'

We reached an inn. He led me in and we sat down together at the table, while he ordered the best wine. And yes, we even shared a cup! Was he trying to make a point, or what, I wondered.

'I just wanted to thank you for showing us all what it means to be human,' he said, with a humility I'd never seen before among his countrymen.

We didn't mention the incident on the road to Jericho. We didn't need to. I just wanted to listen to him and his vision, because if anyone knew about being truly human, it was him.

I guess that's why I'm travelling with him now. To a future without borders. A future without labels.

★ ★ ★

The 'undesirable alien' reminds us vividly of what this pathway is actually about – about becoming human – about choosing, in everyday situations, the more human, the more loving, the more life-giving way to respond.

We have the model of who we are called to be, in Jesus of Nazareth, and there are many other, less celebrated, more limited, models. You will surely know some of them, and could tell your own stories about them. And you might be surprised to discover that some of them see you as a model, in your own way, of what it means to be truly human.

What this story tells us, too, is that these models turn up in the most unlikely places and situations. You may know the story of the man who was walking down the street and noticed a warning sign 'Danger: men working overhead.' In his eagerness to avoid any impact from above, he fell down a manhole at his feet. Sometimes we look for our models in such exalted places that we fail to notice them when they are right in front of us.

Or maybe we do notice them, but don't take them seriously, because they are wearing the 'wrong' label. Jesus had no room at all for people who wanted to fence God in for their own exclusive use, or for people who thought they had 'arrived', and felt free to despise lesser mortals who were still struggling along the way. To such he warned: 'Beware – those who think they are first may end up at the back of the queue! And those whom the world despises will lead the way.' Our 'undesirable alien' is one of them.

Have you come across any unlikely people, who nevertheless modelled something for you of what it means to be human?

Do you wear any 'labels'?

If so, did you choose them, or were they pinned onto you by someone else?

Do you think that labels and borders on the whole help or hinder the quest to become more and more fully human?

Is there anybody in your neighbourhood or workplace who is being treated, implicitly or explicitly, as an 'undesirable alien'? Is there anything you can do to make them feel 'desirable' and welcome?

Have you ever felt like an 'undesirable alien' yourself? If so, what were the circumstances? Who were your friends? What did the experience teach you about what it means to be truly human?

A tale of sound and fury

Before I crashed into him, I was quite literally all over the place. Some people can cope, it seems, with the horrors that are going on all around us. It all seems to run off them like water off a duck's back. Others find their escape in drink or women, or whatever pushes their buttons. Me – I just went to pieces. Everything seemed to be exploding inside me.

No need for a post-mortem – I know there was an unexploded bomb of anger inside me going right back to childhood, and getting more and more lethal every time something new got piled on top of those memories. And there was a huge stockpile of fear too. I got to the point where everything and everybody felt like a threat to my very existence.

There were plenty of objective reasons, sure enough. Events in our land were one long catalogue of oppression and humiliation. We were a people constantly on the edge of revolt. Now, if what I see from 'forever' is anything like true, you would have plenty of reasons of your own to be as frenzied as I once was. Your society seems to be breaking apart as well. All the wealth of the consumer society doesn't make you happy, but only seems to aggravate your discontent. All the money you spend on defence doesn't make you one jot safer, does it? You imagine you can fend off extraterrestrial invaders with your fancy star wars programme, but you can't stop any old guy in jeans and an anorak blowing up your underground trains. But here I go again, forgive me – the old anger dies hard, and truly, I've gone beyond that now.

He found me floundering around on the derelict land outside the city boundary. Folk would leave me well alone out there. No one dared come near me. I was a raging inferno of fury and that gave me an uncanny strength. I thought nothing of wrenching trees up by their roots, and slinging boulders through the air. I could pull a man apart with my bare hands, but, you know what? It was really me, myself, that I wanted to destroy. I hated myself, and I hated the world, just for being there.

He challenged me. I couldn't believe he would dare to walk onto my turf, but there he was. 'What's your name?' he asked. 'Name!' I bellowed back at him, my eyes flashing with malice. 'I don't have a name! Call me "legion" because there's hundreds of me. One for every day of the year, and to spare. Just don't mess with me, that's all!'

But he wasn't having any of it. He just came closer, and I got wilder and wilder, until something snapped. I don't know to this day what he did, but something changed. I stopped in my tracks and he looked straight into my eyes, and I couldn't break the eye contact, however hard I tried.

We both came out of it when we heard a squealing down at the end of the field. Some gremlin had got into a herd of pigs down there, and they were racing headlong towards a cliff.

Jesus took my arm and led me gently back to the village. As we walked, he talked. 'Fear has been driving you,' he explained, 'just like it is driving those pigs over there. It has torn you apart, and your anger has burst at the seams. All that fear and anger was your lower self taking you over. You've been living on your adrenalin, always at war with life, always on the defensive, seeing an enemy in everyone you meet, as if you were still fighting for your existence on the savannah.

'Things can be different now that you understand the reasons. Let the lower self keep to its boundaries. The pigs don't know any better. The lower brain and its fear-driven instincts is all they have. But you have a whole lot more than that to guide you. You can make your life's choices from a higher place than that.'

I wanted to know more. I wanted to follow this man. He had truly put me together again, and I didn't recognise myself. Neither did the folk in the village. They were wary at first – you can imagine – but as time has passed they've got used to me being around, and they've accepted me as one of them. They weren't so sure about Jesus though. I think they blamed him for the pigs going mad. I reckon their own brains were not much clearer than mine.

Sometimes I think it's harder to believe in the best you can be, even when it is standing right there in front of you, like Jesus was that day, than to live with the worst you can be, only one step up from the pigs – and that's being generous!

But I know which I choose now. I was sorry to see him go on his way. He took me beyond my fears and beyond my anger, and gave me the inner space to deal with them both, and see them in perspective. I would have liked to follow him there and then, but he urged me to go home and settle in. I was close to tears as I watched him climb into the boat and take off over the lake. Sad, but ready, too, to start living at a different level altogether.

★ ★ ★

The 'demons' that afflicted our 'angry man' are still very much alive and kicking. If you doubt it, turn on the TV news tonight and see what our civilised world has been up to.

Sometimes the overwhelming weight of what seems like sheer evil in our world feels like it is going to suffocate us. We could so easily slip into the kind of manic fear and fury that possessed the man in the story. Sometimes we do! Or we slide the other way, into the abyss of depression and self-destruction.

Our Guide points us to an inner space where we find a different perspective. When it feels like we are sinking in quicksands, he points towards solid ground on which to base our lives and our decisions.

This isn't going to make the world a better place just like that, but it will give us a rock to stand on, where we can begin to work out what is the more loving thing to do next. If enough of us can do that, it will be the beginning of a change that will spread and gather momentum.

What makes you angry?
Do your feelings lead you into quicksand that drags you down, or towards a solid rock, where you might begin to address the things that inflame your rage?
How might you choose the rock more consciously, and work to avoid the quicksand?

The blind beggar's tale

Jesus was actually my last resort. Anyone who knows me would tell you that I was a career invalid. I've been blind since birth. Some people say my parents must have done something terrible to deserve me – not what I really need to hear! Others say it was me who offended the Almighty and got struck blind as a punishment, but I find it hard to see just what great sin an unborn baby can have committed.

Whatever the reason, as a result of my blindness I've spent my whole life sitting behind my begging bowl. Anything I've eaten has come to me through the begging bowl. My begging bowl has become my alter ego – I can't imagine life without it.

But how I wish I could see! And so I've been the rounds of anyone and everyone who claimed to have healing hands. Some were sympathetic and admitted they couldn't help. Others made grand claims, but never delivered the goods. Most of them simply got fed up with me, and quietly moved on, when I wasn't looking!!

And me? I've spent most of my life ranting at the Almighty: 'Why me?' I've demanded to know of him. 'Why can't you flick the switch for me and get me out of this dark, lonely hole?' Whatever anyone else thought of me, *I* knew I was the grand victim in this black tragi-comedy I call my life. I kind of settled in that part, until I *became* the part, and couldn't think of myself in any other way. My name became 'Poor Me' and I didn't answer to anything else.

Then I heard about this prophet from Galilee who was supposed to be something of a miracle-worker. I decided to give him a go. As I say, he was my last hope … Did I say 'hope'? Did I *really* hope? I don't know. Judge for yourself. But don't come down too hard on me.

I hung around the Temple precincts, hoping I might hear when he was around. I didn't have to wait long. This was my chance. I seized it, and went up to him, boldly asking for one of his miracles for myself. I had nothing to lose, after all … or had I?

I'd heard how he had healed others – even blind folk, and frankly I didn't see why he wouldn't do the same for me. I guess I expected him to lay his hands on my eyes, and speak the magic formula, and hey presto … It wasn't remotely like that.

He listened to my plea all right. I could *feel* him listening. It felt as though every particle of him was focused entirely and exclusively on *me*.

That was such a good feeling. No one had ever done that before. It was almost worth being blind for. When I'd told him my tale, he kicked off by debunking the whole myth of it being either my parents' or my own fault. 'That's not how God is', he thundered. '*When* will people understand?'

Then, turning his attention back to me, he asked me to tell him about myself – what I did all day, and how I felt about things. It didn't take long to tell him how I spend my days. I sit here, me and my begging bowl, and together we listen to the world go by, and especially we listen for the clink of a shekel in the bowl. Enough of those, and that means some dinner tonight. How do I feel about it? What kind of a question was *that*? How did he imagine I would feel about it? I want to see again, of course.

'*Do* you? *Really*?' he interjected.

I was livid. This man was winding me up. What blind beggar wouldn't want to see again? What was that comment supposed to mean?

He must have been reading my thoughts. 'Tell me,' he spoke thoughtfully and slowly. 'Do you want to be healed? Think about what it means to be whole, to see again, to live a normal life. Think. And then tell me truthfully, do you want to be healed?'

I thought! I'd never done that before. I thought of all the things I could do if I had my sight. I could work. I could earn a living. I could participate in the community. I could even think about more intimate relationships … I thought, as he told me to. And you know what – the thoughts appalled me!

Imagine, at my age (I'm no chicken, as you can see), how would I learn a trade? How would I find a job in this ruthless city? Would anyone accept me as a friend or a colleague? Let alone as a husband or lover? Suddenly I wanted to creep right back inside my nice safe shell and stay there. At least as a beggar I had a reasonably steady source of income – meagre, yes, but steady.

Maybe Jesus was watching my reaction. I wouldn't know. But when I'd been going round this loop for quite a while, he interrupted my train of thought. In fact it would be more accurate to say he derailed it!

'Open your eyes,' he commanded, 'and throw your begging bowl away.'

That's what did it. The prospect of parting company with my begging bowl, my alter ego, my only friend. I opened my eyes, sure enough, but no light came in, just tears flowed out.

He caught me in his arms, and held me, while I sobbed out my fears.

'I don't think I could survive outside this little world I live in', I confessed.

'I know,' he calmed me. 'I know, and I tell you, you can, if you want to.'

And that was the miracle. Not exactly what I had in mind, but I knew then that it was a now-or-never choice. I could stay blind, and relatively safe. Or I could have my sight, and all the risk and responsibility of a fuller human life. I felt the strength and the power of his arms holding me. This man was the real McCoy, a fully human being. I knew my choice was made. I wanted to be like him.

I nodded my head.

He placed my begging bowl in my hand and squeezed my arm.

I hurled the bowl away with all the strength I could muster.

I turned to him.

And his eyes were gazing into mine, full of love and power.

He had brown eyes.

I'll never forget them.

★ ★ ★

Is your name ever 'Poor Me'?

(That would be true for most of us, some of the time, so don't be too hard on yourself.)

What form does your personal 'comfort zone' take?

What do you most need from it, and what do you most fear from having to leave it behind?

Which will you choose: to stay safe, or to risk the miracle of transformation?

The fisherman's tale

Even when I was just a little kid I loved messing about in boats. In fact I was a nuisance. The fishermen used to see me coming and try to persuade me to go home to play, but I usually managed to coax one of them to take me out onto the lake.

It was quite a big deal, you know. 'The lake' sounds so harmless, and often it is. But the water is shallow, so when the wind gets up, it really causes mayhem. The winds – and they can be fierce in that part of Galilee – toss the boats around like giants playing with a child's flimsy toy. I'm telling you, you don't want to be out there when one of those sudden storms gets going.

Even as a child I knew the danger, and maybe that's what attracted me so much. To leave the safety of dry land, and risk everything out on the waves – that was the dream that fired me. My friends called me reckless, even then. I thrived on this reputation. To be the one who risked putting out into the great unknown, instead of playing contentedly on the shore, well it gave me a real buzz. I wanted to be different. I wanted to plant my steps where no one had gone before. If I lived in your times, I would be at the front of the queue to join a space mission.

Jesus first crossed my path down on the shore. I was sitting in the boat, mending the nets, and, for once, minding my own business. I noticed a crowd gathering, but didn't take much notice. Then he appeared on the scene. I'd heard about him, but frankly, there were dozens of prophets around who were going to save Israel, so I wasn't all that interested.

I suppose I should tell you how as soon as he started to speak I realised he was different, and dropped everything to follow him. But that's not how it was. No, he could have done his thing there for the crowds, and I would just have gone on mending my nets, I guess. But before he said anything at all, he walked down to the water's edge, and asked if he could use my boat! I was speechless. And anyone who knows me will tell you that doesn't happen very often.

He took my amazed reaction as a 'yes', and stepped right in, a broad smile all over his face, as he muttered his 'Thanks!' And without another word of explanation, he began talking to the crowds, using me and my boat as his floating platform. Somehow it felt like a partnership – and, yes, that's how he treated me all along – like a partner.

I don't know how long he went on talking. In spite of my scepticism,

I was riveted, and so were the people, that was obvious. But if you ask me now what he actually *said*, I couldn't tell you. It was his *presence* that held people, more than his actual words.

Eventually he finished, and the people began to drift off home, but before I could row him back to dry land, his next request came: 'Put out into the deeper water.'

He wasn't joking. From that moment on, my whole life has been 'in deeper water'. In fact I've been in it over my ears. I just didn't know what hit me. His request left no room for a 'No'. I did as he asked, turned the boat out towards the horizon, and rowed out into the deep.

Well, I could tell you hundreds of stories about what happened after that. From that day on my life and his were intertwined. But you asked me why I'm here walking this path, and whether I really believe there is 'another lake' – something more than we can imagine beyond the horizon of our human understanding. So let me tell you about another encounter on that same lake, several years later.

It was a foul night. The winds were already gusting. Jesus had once again been speaking to a vast crowd of people, and it had got late, and dark. When they had finally all dispersed, he had gone off to the hills to be alone, and gather his thoughts. He often did that. It was the still place where he drew his own life's energy. He told us to go on ahead across the lake, and he would catch up with us.

But the winds were against us. It was crazy really to set out in that little boat, but we trusted him, and when he said he was coming after us, we believed him, though, thinking about it, that promise didn't make any kind of sense. After a few hours we were really in trouble. The storm was full on by then, and the boat was tossing around like a cork. We were frankly scared out of our wits. We ran around like headless chickens, everyone trying to do something practical to keep us afloat, but we all knew it was hopeless.

At moments like that, so they say, you see your whole life passing in front of you like a video in fast forward. I know that I thought my hour had come. It was truly the worst hour of my life. The fear took me over. I became the fear. I didn't know what I was doing.

And it was exactly at this zero-hour in my life that I saw him coming towards me, across the stormy waters. I saw him stretch out his hands. I heard him calling '*Don't be afraid.*' I plunged over the edge of the boat, and knew I had to walk towards him out there on the water.

Ironic? Me, the one who always wanted to tread where none had trod before, and here was he, doing exactly that. Here was the one who could leave footprints on water … I sank, of course! Or I would have done, but at the last moment he seized my arm and hauled me out.

The storm subsided – inside and outside.

I wish I could just leave it there, and tell you 'he saved me'. That would make a much neater, cleaner story. And you could trust then that he will save you, and all will be well. And that would be true, but there was more to it than that, much more. That night on the water was only a beginning – another beginning.

I was going to sink a whole lot more, before I really understood who he is, and what his call means.

He kept his promise that night. He caught up with us. He saved us. After that he walked ahead of us, through hell and high water. The 'saving' was only the beginning. But did I tell you that that night on the lake was the worst hour of my life? I was wrong.

The day came when he needed 'saving' himself. It was another foul night. It felt like all the darkness in creation was gathered to swallow us up. They arrested him, and took him off, and we all knew the dream was over. Oh, I wanted to be the hero then. I would have done anything, or so I thought, to change the course of history. But instead I fled into the darkness. When the going got tough, I pretended I'd never known him! If Jesus and I had ever been 'in partnership', I had breached the contract completely and irrevocably. Yes, the big adventurer in me turned out to be a miserable cringing coward, and how I hated myself. I'd been untrue to the best that life can be. The only alternative was to be the worst. I fell into despair and self-loathing.

When you don't know how to keep on living, you go back to the only thing you know how to do. After the events of that night and what followed, I went fishing. Not that I caught anything. My dream had turned into a nightmare, and even the fish had fled, just like I did!

I remembered the last supper we had shared together, the Passover supper. If only I could turn back time, I thought. But time is never for turning back. The river of life always moves forwards. I should have known that he would always be that river, always moving forwards, always calling me forwards, calling all of us forwards.

I didn't recognise him at first. Well, I was hardly expecting to see him, given that only days earlier he had been executed! Even when he waved me over to the shore, I didn't recognise him. Even when he invited me to join him for a breakfast barbecue.

How do I know it was him?

When he broke the loaf for us, I knew I had known those hands.

When he said '*Don't be afraid*', I knew I had known that voice.

When he looked into my eyes, and said 'Peter, do you love me?' I knew …

★ ★ ★

Does anything in the fisherman's story resonate with your own experience?

Have you ever been untrue to the best in yourself?

How do you feel now about the 'partnership' you have with life, and with the best that life is calling us into?

Have you ever been through experiences that felt, at the time, that they were destroying you?

How did you choose to react?

Did they actually destroy you?

How do you feel about them now?

An unfinished tale

I don't know where to begin. Where do you begin a story that you know you can never finish?

I think I need to start at the end, because the end, of course, was only a new beginning.

I'd staked my life on this man. I was utterly convinced that he was going to change the world, and I was thrilled beyond words to be a part of it all. How I ever became a part of it all still amazes me. You see, I was in the pits. I'd been on the edge for years. The edge of polite society. The edge of respectability. I wasn't the kind of girl nice men really wanted to know.

But he *did*. He wanted to know. He bothered to ask how things were with me. He was interested in my story. He noticed me when everyone else looked straight through me. And the thing was, he cared for the *real* me. He wasn't after a 'good time'.

I laugh at myself now for even using that phrase 'a good time'. Back then I used to think a 'good time' meant a night out on the town, too much to drink, and a bed with anyone who offered themselves. If anyone had told me then that there was something way better than that, and that if I wanted it I would find it following a dream along stony roads, never quite knowing where the next meal would turn up – well, I'd have curled up laughing.

We became close friends. He was the only man who'd ever given me a sense of my own worth, and yet he never once abused the friendship. I learned from him that a true friend is worth a hundred lovers.

And then they killed him.

My world ended. This had been the truest person who ever walked this earth. If you want to know what 'human being' means, he was it. He never once harmed a single soul. Quite the opposite. He had healing hands. He brought people back home to themselves. He gave life. You could feel it, radiating out from him all the time. He told us stories that made sense of so much that was wrong with our lives and made us long to follow the dream along with him.

And it was a dream with feet, not some airy-fairy pie-in-the-sky stuff that makes you behave on earth so that you'll get a place in heaven. He wasn't having any of that. For him, 'heaven' was already a seed growing and sprouting on earth, in everyday life, all around us. All we needed to do, he said, was open our eyes to see, and our ears to hear. I remember how he once told us 'The kingdom of heaven is very close to you. It's written in your own heart.'

But the darkness can't stand the light. His words and deeds upset too many apple-carts. Too many people felt their own empires were threatened by his simple message of love and peace. Too many people had a vested interest in keeping things as they were. God help us, they thought, if the ordinary folk start finding God for themselves.

And even the ordinary folk that he loved so much, even they joined in the clamour at the end. He told us we were eagles, and showed us how to fly. And we chose to stay in the chicken run, grubbing around for a meal each day, until we were fat enough to land on someone's dinner plate. Yes, he offered us the mountain tops, and we chose the chicken run.

We killed him. He disturbed us too much.

It was three days later. I went to the place they had buried him, to spend some time with my memories. I just wanted to sink into my sorrow, and never come up again.

I couldn't find him! Can you believe it? The man who spent all his life searching for us and finding us, couldn't be found. How does a dead man go missing? I was beside myself. I'd lost him, irrevocably, on Friday, and now, on Sunday, I'd lost him all over again.

I saw the gardener and asked him where I might find the body. At first I thought the man was stupid, or deaf. He just looked at me with an expression that seemed to say 'Isn't it obvious?'

Then he said something. He spoke my name … 'Mary …'

Suddenly I was right back at the beginning, when we first met, and he'd spoken to me in that same infinitely gentle tone, and called me 'Mary'. It was a first for me. Other people just called me 'Woman'. 'Woman, come over here a while.' 'Woman, fetch me another drink.' 'Woman, my bed is waiting for you.'

He called me 'Mary', right from the word go.

My heart just flooded. Here he was. And the whole thing on Friday had been a bad dream. We could forget the nightmare and go back to where we were as if nothing had happened. I wanted to fall at his feet and hold fast, and tell him how much I loved him. He stopped me.

'Mary', he said. 'We can't ever go back. The way leads only forward. Don't hang on to the past, however good it was for us. The future draws us on. The future has such gifts for us, but we can't receive them unless we move on with empty hands.'

'Are you asking me to let you go, now that I've found you?' I whispered.

'I'm inviting you to travel with me,' he replied, 'to a future we are shaping together. The paths to that future are not found but made, and the making of those pathways changes both the traveller and the destination.'

Are you coming, or staying where you are?

How the tale continues is up to you.

Fly or die?

Are you coming, or staying where you are? How the tale continues is up to you …

What if these words were not just addressed to Mary, in our last story, but also to you personally?

And what if they are not just addressed to you personally, but to the whole human family, the whole of *homo sapiens*?

How will we respond?

And does it actually matter how we respond?

Does it make any difference?

Remember the eagle and the chicken in our last story?

What if we, individually, and as a whole human family, are like a chick, fluttering around in the early stages of our story, not yet knowing who we are, or where we might be headed?

The Guide says this chick is an eagle, destined to soar to the mountaintops, and see a vision beyond the horizon. The Guide says it's worth letting go of everything else to become that eagle and fly to all we can become. It's worth letting go of the apparent safety and comfort of our present way of life. It's worth saying 'goodbye' to the chicken run, and risking the flight. He doesn't just say it. He lives it. He dies for it. And he transcends all we are, to become all we can be.

But the 'world', our familiar life patterns and expectations, our culture and our lesser selves hold back. The risk is too great. The future is unknown. We may lose everything if we let the Guide overturn our assumptions about how things are. We feel safer in our fears than with our dreams. The 'world' says this chick is only a chicken, and its destiny is to cluck around the chicken run, scrabbling for food, fighting for its corner and its share of the birdseed. What the 'world' forgets to tell us is that the chicken is destined for nothing more than the dinner plate, when it gets fat enough. And meanwhile we content ourselves with getting fatter and fatter …

We can choose to stay in the chicken run. Many species have done that before us. But they didn't have the potential to do anything else. We do. We have bigger brains, and expanding spirits, and hearts capable of compassion and love and of dreaming big dreams, and we have the Guide to model the way and empower the onward journey. We can choose the inevitable extinction that we face if we stay on our present tracks. Or we can choose the mountaintops.

In the final part of our journey, we will spread our wings, and fly over some of the landscape of our times, and see what it might mean to choose the eagle's wings.

Feel free to stay in the terminal, and reflect on what 'terminal' might mean,

Or to board the flight …

THE EDGE OF THE NEST

'More powerful than any army is an idea whose time has come.'

Victor Hugo

Sky dive

It was a peaceful Sunday morning. We were just sitting quietly over our morning tea, when the phone rang. From the other side of the world an excited voice bubbled out all over the kitchen. 'I'm so thrilled,' she told us. 'I've just jumped out of an aeroplane from twelve thousand feet, and you wouldn't believe how amazing it all is …'

Our daughter fell over herself in her eagerness to share her news with us. She was a student, backpacking her way around the world, and her journey had so far brought her to New Zealand, where she had had a go at sky-diving – a piece of information we appreciated receiving *after* the event and not before!

Later, when she returned home and shared more of her feelings about this adventure, she told us of how overwhelmed she had felt by the awesome beauty she was witnessing as she drifted down to earth, safely strapped to an instructor, and held aloft by a parachute – the deep stillness of the rain forests, the icy splendour of the glaciers, the restless motion of the sea.

'Weren't you scared at all?' I asked her in wonderment.

'Everything was fine,' she admitted, 'until they opened the door and I had to jump!'

I was reminded of this episode several years later on a lovely summer evening in the medieval city of York. After supper I went for a stroll along the riverside, and to my surprise and amusement, I found myself heading straight into a column of several hundred geese, all walking in formation (more or less) to some destination they had obviously all agreed on.

Eventually they all reached a ramp that led down to the river, and I watched them take to the water. One family had a brood of several small goslings, all of whom, with some encouragement, flopped into the water and swam after their parents. But the last one was afraid. He just wasn't going in there. The parents and siblings rallied round, and by means of a combination of friendly encouragement and brute force, they persuaded him to take the plunge, and they all swam off together happily into the sunset.

Eagles, I understand, have their own methods of coaxing the fledgling chicks over the edge of the nest. Apparently they build their nests high in the cliffs, on a base of hard rock. The first layer of the family home comprises rough stones and twigs. Then comes a layer of moss or leaves. Finally comes the 'duvet' of softer materials, perhaps even the feathers from the parents' own bodies. Into this nest they lay their eggs.

When the eggs have hatched, and the time comes for the little ones to learn to fly, the parents sometimes have to persuade them to leave the comforts of home. If any of the chicks seems set to stay put in the nest for ever, the parents first remove the topmost soft layer. If that doesn't do the trick, the next layer, of leaves and moss, is jettisoned. Usually by the time the reluctant fledgling is down to the 'stone floor', it gets the message, and tries its wings.

And what a moment that must be: imagine these little birds teetering on the edge of the nest, high up in the mountains, with an awful lot of empty space between them and the earth far, far below. It must take a huge amount of courage to make that first flight, not really knowing how it will feel, or how to use your wings.

But what parent is actually going to let their offspring fall to certain death, should the first flight prove abortive? And so, the story goes, the parent eagle actually flies below the chick, ready to catch it on her own wings, in case of an emergency.

We, the human family, are still tiny fledglings quivering on the brink of all our tomorrows. We hover on the edge of the nest, dreading the loss of its safety, yet knowing too that growth demands of us a courageous response to this new stage of our becoming.

Our daughter's skydiving adventure (as well as the little goslings) taught me some important lessons:

- She had no more idea about how to do it, than I have. The jump was only possible because she was securely strapped to an experienced parachutist.
- She had to overcome a considerable barrier of fear when the door of the plane was opened and there was no alternative but to jump.
- To be able to jump, she needed to put her trust completely in her guide. The trust had to be stronger than the fear.
- When she was able to let herself fall, a breathtaking new vision opened up to her – something she could never have seen from ground level.

The time has come to take to our wings, spiritually.

As a human family destined, we believe, to evolve beyond all we think we are or can be, we are invited to risk the flight of life on our untried wings. We can only do this because we have been nurtured in a good 'nest'. The nest is where our deep roots are and where they always will be. The nest has been our place of growth thus far. We have been cradled in the story of life itself and nourished by the source of that life. That same life now calls us to fly forth – but not alone. Can we believe, and trust, that we will be held as securely in our flight as we have been in the nest? What does the 'flight' mean for us, and what new visions await us if we risk the leap?

Jesus of Nazareth left us an *idea* – the best and brightest Idea that humanity ever had! The 'idea of becoming fully human', and in doing so, to become truly a reflection of the divine. He planted the idea among us because its time had come.

Its time is still coming.

Its time is now.

It has more power than all the armies in the world, yet it is as gentle as a baby's sigh.

When an idea's time has come, it begins to bubble up all over the place. People from widely different backgrounds start to explore it in very different ways. They start to notice that they are not alone. They start to talk to each other. They are amazed at the resonance they discover. No one 'owns' the idea. It has a life of its own. But all are invited to participate in bringing it to birth.

Perhaps our 'flight' is nothing less than the bringing to birth of this Idea, each of us in our own way and according to our own gifts and experiences.

And Jesus, who both heralds and empowers this birthing, is also the one to whom we are securely strapped as we jump from the plane. He promises to be with us always as we walk the 'narrow way'. He holds us in our flight and opens up the new vision. He is the midwife, urging and encouraging our own participation in the bringing to birth of the future through our own life's circumstances and choices. As we take flight, we will listen especially to some of the things he had to say to guide us more deeply into the adventure of becoming fully human.

What does this idea mean to you?
Do you want to be a part, yourself, of the bubbling-up of this Idea whose time has come, perhaps by sharing your thoughts and feelings with other spiritual explorers …?

Where do you think we are headed?
How do you think we might navigate the future?
What skills do we need?
And what visions open up to us,
　　　　as we take the risk
　　　　　　　of flight?

A bird's-eye view

There is something fascinating about watching the land mass spread out beneath you as you gradually rise from the tarmac, before the plane passes through the cloud cover, and the view is obscured. It's a bird's-eye view, and it makes a good starting point as we explore some of the light and shadows of our soul's flight.

Another 'bird's-eye view' that we see most evenings is the TV weather map, revealing what life holds for us, weather-wise, over the coming days.

There was a bit of a furore in the United Kingdom, when the BBC changed the design of its weather maps. Scotland, particularly, felt side-lined, and it was true that because of the strange perspective, the vast tracts of Scotland looked, on the map, like a small northern peninsula, while the heavy 'foot' of southern England dominated the whole show. I'm happy to report that the BBC changed its design promptly, and the present weather maps show a much-improved balance.

But they show a lot more than this. Obviously the design gurus think we are losing the ability either to read or to listen, and so the weather maps are overwhelmingly pictorial. When you look at them you can see fairly easily where it is going to be sunny (nice light, bright patches), where it is going to be cloudy (dark, broody patches) and where it is going to rain (blue blotches). And you can see the predicted temperatures and wind strengths.

Jesus once admonished his friends for being able to read the weather forecast from the clouds, but failing to 'read the signs of the times'. If we imagine ourselves flying over the landscape of the twenty-first century the view may reveal something of our 'spiritual weather'. What *are* the signs of the times? In what ways is humanity moving towards the light? Where is it still in the fog? Where are refreshing rains falling? Where is there spiritual drought? From which direction are the winds of change blowing, and what do they portend? And does our heart-map fall into the same error of perspective that first beset the BBC? Are we focusing too heavily on some aspects of life and sidelining others?

Let's spend a few minutes flying over our heart's terrain, and see what we notice. Or, more accurately, see what *you* notice. Because your obser-vations don't have to be the same as mine, and what matters here is for you to see for yourself how things are looking to *you*. I share my own view of the terrain only as a way of inviting you to observe for yourself how things are, and to draw your own conclusions. What matters is that *all* of us, the human family, feel free and welcome to share in a lively debate and a thoughtful reflection about how we are evolving, and whether we are happy with what we see. Every voice matters. Every thought counts.

Sunny intervals

Where do you see the bright patches on our spiritual weather map?

A few suggestions:

The growing awareness that we are a global family. Ordinary people, for example, respond with overwhelming generosity to appeals for help from parts of the world that are struggling to deal with natural disaster or the aftermath of war.

The growing voice of popular protest against armed intervention and the use of military force.

The quest for a spiritual dimension in life. Millions of people, including very many who would not call themselves 'religious', are searching for the depths of the mystery we might call God.

Growing and active concern for the well-being of the planet, and the realisation that we are participants in life, not its masters.

The growing desire for a simpler, more wholesome lifestyle, and disillusionment with the 'consumer society' and the accumulation of 'things' for their own sake.

The wide range of individuals and action groups working for justice and peace in specific areas of human activity, and seeking to shine an ethical spotlight on the activities of various institutions.

Cloudy and overcast

And the dark patches? Where are they hovering?

Some possibilities:

A widespread breakdown in *trust*. For a variety of reasons, many of them very valid, we have lost the confidence we once had in almost all our institutions, including politics, the professions, the media and the Church. This may be suggesting that humanity as a whole is moving towards new, and less institutional ways of managing its affairs, but it also brings with it the danger of a breakdown in trust of humanity as a whole and of ourselves personally.

The insidious power of the consumer markets, of multinational corporations and of the media to shape our choices in life and to mould our values into what is profitable for *them*.

A sense of despair that drives us into artificial ways of coping with life, such as drugs, casual sex, 'retail therapy', and any number of other compulsions.

The grip of fear, and the willingness to sacrifice freedom and natural human interaction for the sake of security, both national and personal.

The rising tide of substance addiction and violent crime, suggesting huge and dangerous forces of unprocessed anger and frustration just underneath the surface of our lives.

Refreshing rain

In these islands rain is such a frequent visitor that it is rarely welcomed, except, in summer, by gardeners. What about our spiritual rainfall?

Heavy showers of doubt and disillusionment have fallen upon our postmodern, post-Christian world. These deluges have caused dismay and disorientation, but they have also washed away much of the old surface coating of unquestioning acceptance that kept us obedient to various forms of imposed authority in the past. While this can feel uncomfortable and even threatening, it may provide a necessary cleansing and refreshment.

The downpour that has washed away the sand on which some of our castles of faith and parts of our social order were built has, at least potentially, exposed deeper bedrock that offers us a much more secure, though far less comfortable basis for our spiritual lives. They have made us think for ourselves about big questions, rather than simply reciting the official answers. They have forced us to accept some responsibility ourselves for how things are in our society, and be more willing to enter into debate and action for change. In some respects they have stirred us into our true prophetic calling to challenge what we perceive to be morally wrong in the way things are, both in church and state and in our smaller circles of influence.

Rain usually feels like bad news when it starts to fall, but afterwards we can often see, if we choose to look, that it has nourished our growth. This is the case with some of the very terrible events of recent years. In the wake of disaster, human beings turn to each other, and bonds can be strengthened.

Are we going to hide under our umbrellas, or allow the rain to be a gift that cleanses and renews us?

Winds of change

A prominent feature on our spiritual weather map right now would be some strong winds. These are the winds of change. Some are just a bit blustery. Others are typhoon strength. Some are bringing good change.

Some are rocking the boat and threatening us with shipwreck. How do we tell the difference, and what can we do about it?

We are living in 'interesting times' – so it is often said. 'Interesting times' are difficult times, times of enormous challenge, times during which humanity is at a crossroads. We are in the midst of a major paradigm shift. The old order is breaking down and the new order is not remotely apparent. The 'nest' of our former certainties is getting uncomfortable. In every aspect of life, these 'certainties' are being questioned. Can the events of two thousand years ago provide a key to take us beyond chaos to a new creation?

The Genesis writer gives us a picture of how once the life-generating energy we call the Spirit of God hovered over the primordial chaos, the quantum soup from which life, in all its complexity, would emerge. Can we trust that this same Spirit is hovering over our collective chaos of heart, mind and soul on planet Earth today? Can the Christic vision that emerged into the world two thousand years ago, be the key to the 'new order', the 'new age', or as Jesus described it, 'the new covenant'?

We can probably name some of the winds blowing through our twenty-first century lives: warm and life-giving winds might include the breath of compassion sometimes stirred up by catastrophe and suffering in different parts of the world. But a cold and powerful wind bears down upon us in the form, for example, of religious fundamentalism that seeks to turn back the clock and seduce us into false 'securities' and fosters adversarial confrontation between different faith traditions.

A matter of perspective

The BBC got itself into trouble, you remember, for the initially unbalanced perspective of the weather map. The distortions in perspective on our spiritual maps may not be at all obvious, and perhaps precisely for that reason they can seriously mislead us.

The maps of what constitutes 'the right way to live', that we have been using for centuries past, have had a heavy loading towards external religious practice, church-going, strict denominational affiliation, keeping the rules and behaving well enough on earth to get to heaven after death. You could have been forgiven for looking at the 'map' and thinking this was what Christianity was all about.

Questions surrounding the spiritual search, the possibility of seeking God in new and personal ways and applying gospel values to everyday life, discovering the common ground between all searchers and all faith traditions, and embracing the demands that faith makes for justice and peace at a practical level were very much peripheral to 'religion' in general.

The perspective is changing. Enough people have noticed the distortion and are taking steps to correct it. The map is changing quite rapidly and dramatically. Some might say that we are moving beyond 'maps' altogether ...?

What do you feel?

Where do you see the areas of light?
Where do you feel the clouds are gathering?
Are the rains refreshing us or swamping us?

Where are the winds of change blowing?
Which of them are helpful, which are harmful?

How do you feel humanity's 'spiritual map' is changing?
For some people, the apparent lack of definitive 'maps' for right living feels like liberation; for others it looks like anarchy. How do you feel? What does your map look like?

On the flight deck

Over the centuries, those who have been walking the way pioneered by the Guide have accumulated some wisdom that can help us all. They have noticed what helps them stay on course and what keeps them true to the values Jesus embodies. The Guide himself has become, in his own words 'the way'. Perhaps a living 'way' supersedes the need for the maps we used to walk by?

Jesus, as we have seen, left us an idea – an idea whose time has come. He also left us some very high *ideals*. Much of what he is reported to have said to his friends while he lived on earth sounds so idealistic that most of us feel we could never live true to it.

It has been said that 'ideals are like the stars; we never reach them, but like the mariners of the sea, we chart our course by them'. The ideals that Jesus lives out for us are like that. We are very far from being able to live true to them ourselves, but we *can* plot our course by them.

He urged his friends to '*learn from me*'.

What tools would we need to be able to do this?

Here are some items you might find useful for your inflight toolkit:

Silence and stillness

Times of silence and solitude were very important to the Guide, and he urges us to make space for them in our own lives. In stillness our hearts become receptive to the quiet whispers of the eternal mystery. Until and unless we are receptive to these invisible stirrings deep within us, we cannot hope to live true to them. What we hear in the silence we can turn into wisdom for our living. This is the art of ...

Reflective living

Socrates said, 'the unexamined life is not worth living'. Why would that be? One reason, perhaps, is that reflection is a means of turning raw experience into wisdom. Experience is something we all have. Every moment of our lives we are experiencing events, relationships and situations that are new to us, but we will only learn from this experience if we take time to *reflect* on it. We can do this just by looking back over the events of our days, noticing how we reacted, reflecting on anything that is to be learned from the process, and then putting that new wisdom into action in our living. To do this effectively, we need to develop a ...

Friendship with the Guide
The Guide is the one who reveals the ideals we are hoping to steer our
course by.There is only one way to find out the real nature of these ideals
and that is by getting to know the Guide. This means getting to know
him with our hearts, not just our heads, entering into intimate relationship *with* him, not just studying the records *about* him.Yet the records *are*
important.We *do* have four separate accounts of who this man was, how
he lived and what he taught.We can nourish our personal friendship with
him by 'getting inside' these accounts, thinking ourselves into the situations they describe, and making connections between what we find there
and the particular situations and relationships we are dealing with in our
own lives. In doing so we are not searching for the definitive facts about
his life, but we are seeking to incorporate *his values and attitudes* into our
own hearts, choices and decisions.To do this, we need to ...

Stay focused
If you have ever had the opportunity to watch the conductor of an
orchestra or choir from the perspective of the musicians themselves (rather
than that of the audience), you will see that he or she is not just someone
waving a stick.The conductor is constantly drawing the disparate members
of the orchestra or choir into the music at exactly the right moment,
encouraging them continually, restraining them occasionally, and doing all
of this out of a hugely inspiring love of the music and all those who are
making it.A good conductor totally lives the music, and enthuses everyone
in the orchestra to do the same for their own part of the score.And at the
end of the performance, it is the conductor who urges the musicians to rise
and receive the applause and affirmation of the audience.

     This is a far cry from, say, the military commander who barks his
orders out from above and punishes anyone who fails to comply. The
military commander demands blind obedience. The conductor invites
focused and sensitive awareness.

     The Guide is a bit like a fine conductor, inviting each of us, at exactly
the right moment, to contribute our unique note to the symphony of life.
All we are asked to do is keep our attention, our hearts and minds,
focused on him and listen for, and respond to, his every move within us.
How do we do this? One way might be to ...

Nourish what humanises us; starve what dehumanises us
There will always be aspects of our lives and ourselves that we know are
making us into more fully human people, and other aspects that we know
are tending to dehumanise us.We can't choose our circumstances, or even
our personalities and tendencies, but we *can* choose how we react to

whatever happens to us. Using the skills of reflectiveness, we can learn to be more sensitive to the various movements in our hearts in response to events in our lives, and we can actively choose to give our attention to those things that are tending towards life. What we nourish will grow. What we starve will shrink. Which parts of ourselves do we want to grow? Sifting our experience to discover what is life-giving, not just for ourselves but for all creation, and what is life-diminishing, is the basis of …

Discernment

'Discernment' is simple. It's just about choosing the best! Or, rather, it's about letting the 'best' in us do the choosing, in all the situations life flings at us.

And discernment is incredibly hard, because there is so much pressure from all that is less than the best in us, and all that is less than good in humanity generally, to do the opposite, and to focus only on our own gain or comfort, at the expense of the rest of creation. Remember how the 'good branch' and the 'bad branch' have become so entangled that we are very hard-pressed to see which one we are sitting on at any given moment.

Nevertheless, discernment is one of our greatest gifts and most effective tools for life. It is an art that grows with us and helps us, increasingly, to make our choices – both little and large – from the true centre of ourselves, in spite of all the nudgings to the contrary from the 'lower brain'. We can help discernment to grow and flourish in us by asking ourselves the questions: 'In this situation what is the more life-giving, the more loving thing to do next? What would the Guide's attitude be? What does the best in me choose?'

Which helps you more:

To think of the ideals set out by Jesus as the standard you have to reach, and to see yourself as 'sinning' every time you fall short of them, or

To think of these ideals as stars in your heart that have been given to you to help you steer your course through life in a way that makes you, and all of us, a bit more fully human?

The story of two wolves

Once upon a time there was a wise old Native American grandfather. He had a beloved little grandson. Each night he would take his grandson onto his lap and tell him a bedtime story. The child's favourite story was this:

'In every human heart,' his grandfather would tell him, 'there are two wolves. One wolf is about all the things we wish we were, all the things we value in ourselves and each other: the generosity, the compassion, the courage, the gentleness, and so on. The other wolf is about all the things we dislike in ourselves, and wish we could overcome: the jealousy, the resentment, the deceitfulness, the greed, and so on. These two wolves prowl around in our hearts all the time and are in conflict with one another until the day we die.'

'But, Grandad,' interrupted the little boy, 'which wolf wins?'

And Grandad replied: 'The one that you feed.'

★ ★ ★

One little tool you might like to keep handy as you start to fly to all that you can become is this simple question:

In this situation, here and now, which wolf am I feeding?

Rising high – but where to?

We sense that our human flight is headed towards what Irenaeus, a second-century Christian theologian, has called 'the human being fully alive' – the fully-evolved human being who perfectly reflects the divine source of life. The wise ones of the past suggest this, and our own evolutionary story confirms this pattern. Christians believe that we see this fully evolved, fully alive person embodied in Jesus of Nazareth.

Yet, if you were to take your cue from our western culture and its media and advertising influence, or even from some of the more serious voices of modern science and technology, you might come to the conclusion that we are well set on a course towards becoming *superhuman* in our own, very different way. Is this what we mean by 'fully alive'? Or is it a seductive distraction?

We've noticed how our long evolutionary story takes us through the stage of being 'just body' and part of the food chain, to being 'body plus mind', and therefore creatures of reason, capable of making choices, through to being 'body plus mind plus spirit', creatures capable of reflecting on our own origins and destiny and the nature and power of the mystery in whom we live and move and have our being.

The lure of the superhuman might follow this pattern too.

For example, it might be telling us that our destiny lies in perfecting the *physical* nature of our being. This could involve:

- Trying to achieve the perfect body, by dieting or by more drastic, surgical methods.
- Trying to conquer all known disease and correct any biological imperfections, through conventional or alternative medicine, and, more radically, through genetic engineering.
- Trying to delay physical death indefinitely, for example by perfecting organ transplant and artificial life support.

Or it might be telling us that our destiny lies in perfecting the *mental and intellectual* nature of our being, for example by:

- Developing super computers, artificial intelligence and robotics.
- Emphasising the importance of academic training of our young, possibly at the cost of other aspects of their personalities.

Or it may be telling us that our destiny lies in *spiritual* perfection, which, though it sounds worthy, is also prone to distortion, such as:

- Focusing on keeping sets of rules and behaving in such a way on earth as to ensure for ourselves a place in 'heaven'.
- Focusing entirely on our own personal spiritual fulfilment, without seeing ourselves as part of an interrelated and interdependent created order.

These are some of the voices of our contemporary culture. They urge us towards aspects of progress that are in many ways very good things in themselves, but are they the voice of our true destiny? Do they echo the values of our Guide? Are they really making us more human?

The Guide once invited his friends to take a good long look at the flowers growing in the fields. Then he asked them the question: 'Do you really think that, even if you put all your effort into achieving it, you can actually make yourselves grow a few inches taller? Look at the flowers – they don't have any hang-ups about achieving anything, and yet they continue to thrive there in the field. Why do you put such enormous effort into trying to make yourselves bigger, stronger, more beautiful, or even longer-lived. That's really not the point.'

The flowers of the field become fully what they are just by growing into their fullness. They do almost nothing to enable this process, but there *is* one they have to do, to allow the process to begin. They have to surrender the safety of the seed. They have to let that fragile little shell rot away in the darkness of the earth, or be consumed by an animal, or be carried on a creature's fur to some unknown place, perhaps far from home. Their miraculous growth begins not in acquiring some skill or superiority, but in *letting go* of the little they have.

If we trust the wisdom of the Guide, therefore, the way ahead for humanity lies not so much in all the great things we think we can achieve, laudable though these may be in themselves, but in our will-ingness to let go of what we think makes us so secure, and trust the uncertainty of a destiny that calls us beyond ourselves.

When Jesus died, his last words from the cross are reported to have been: 'It is finished', 'It is completed'. Jesus had broken through to the full-ness of his, and our, destiny, not by hanging on but by letting go. In doing so, he opened up the way to a future that is unimaginable from where we are standing.

Sometimes this breakthrough experience can be glimpsed in our world too. I think, for example, of the reactions of the human family especially in the shadow of great tragedy. During the Second World War, it is said, the British people (and undoubtedly the people of other nations too) discovered a much deeper and less selfish way of relating to each other and ministering to each other's needs. In the aftermath of the Asian tsunami the heart of the world was mobilised in a dramatic way to reach out in love and support to the victims of the disaster.

At an individual level we sometimes see how people who have suffered violent crime or devastating disease come fighting back, in such a spirit of resilience and surge of life that thousands of others are inspired by their mere presence. Or we encounter people who have suffered abuse, injustice or betrayal, yet find a way forward not through revenge but through compassion. This is the *genuinely* 'superhuman' peeping through our defences. It isn't about superiority of body or of mind or even of spirit. It is about openness of *heart*. And, paradoxically, we see it through our weakness, not in our strength.

Imagine the feelings of an unborn child, still in the womb, but coming close to the time for delivery. At present the child is in the perfect 'comfort zone'. The temperature is just right, the placental food supply is consistent and reliable, and mum's heartbeat ticks away reassuringly in the background. Then the contractions begin. The baby is systematically, and painfully, squeezed out of its only home. If it could express its feelings, it might say that it is about to lose its home, its food supply and even its mother – the only person it has ever 'known'.

The child is born. The home is gone. The midwife promptly and ruthlessly cuts off the food supply, and the child – predictably – bawls! It has yet to discover that in losing a very limited 'home', it has inherited the whole Earth to be its domain. In losing the placental food supply it has come into a kingdom of an infinite variety of new tastes and textures. And in 'losing' its mother, it has entered into the beginning of a whole new and infinitely deeper relationship with her, and with a multitude of other people too. But all these things remain to be discovered in this new phase of being that is just beginning.

The same is true for us, as we teeter on the brink of this transition from where and who we are to all that we might be destined to become. We think we have everything to lose, and we must cling grimly to all we can salvage of 'the old'. In fact, we have everything to gain, but the gain is only there for those who approach the future with empty hands and a trusting heart.

In what ways do you feel that our restless striving to become 'superhuman' may be distracting us from our true destiny to become fully evolved, fully alive persons?

Where do you see evidence of the evolution of the heart of humankind towards a new compassion and openness?

Buried treasure in a muddy field

The Guide once told his friends this story:

Once upon a time there lived a man who spent his whole life searching for an elusive buried treasure. He travelled everywhere in search of it,
asked all the world's wisest people where he might find it, and spent all
his energy in the search for it.

One day, when he had almost given up the quest, he was trudging
across a muddy field, feeling a bit despondent. All at once he glanced
down and noticed that the toe of his boot had turned up the soil and
something was glittering there in the mud. He bent down, and picked up
the shiny particle. He couldn't believe his own eyes. Here, hidden in the
middle of this filthy field was buried treasure.

Quickly he covered the treasure with soil again, and ran back to town.
He put together all his life savings, and went to the merchant who owned
the field where the treasure lay. He spent every penny he owned to pur-
chase the field. He gave up everything, to gain the elusive treasure, for his
heart told him it was worth more than all he owned.

★ ★ ★

How much will we pay for the heart-treasure that we long for?
Is anything holding us back?
The greatest obstacle between us and our heart-treasure is the arch-
enemy of our souls:

fear ...

Hitting the turbulence

'Serial killer at large!' When we hear words like this on the news programmes we immediately switch to survival mode, keep our children in,
lock our doors and windows and become extremely watchful. We wonder whether everyone we see might be 'the one'. We become suspicious
of everything and our energies are focused upon self-preservation. A
noise in the night can make our stomachs lurch. An unguarded moment
might be our last.

Fear has moved in, and taken over …

In today's world there is always a serial killer lurking around somewhere. It may be the bored but enterprising IT student who circulates his
computer virus. It may be the guy we thought was an ordinary neighbour, who turns out to have been a suicide bomber. Or it may be
something much less tangible even than these: the fear of the final
demand for the bills we can't pay; the fear of advancing age and frailty that
makes us so vulnerable in a world that is owned by the young and the
strong or the fear of being alone and insecure in a world that seems so
confident and won't stand still to wait for us to catch up. Fear has a
thousand faces.

In the BBC Reith Lectures for 2004 the Nobel prize winning poet,
playwright, and courageous opponent of dictatorship, Wole Soyinka,
reminded us that sixty years ago the face of fear was that of a manic tyrant
who wanted to rule the world. Forty years ago it was the face of nuclear
annihilation. Today it is the face of terrorism. If we could go back far
enough, we would surely see that for as long as *homo sapiens* has roamed
the earth, fear has roamed with him.

Today we can almost bury the memory of Hitler, and consign him to
history. It wasn't so in 1940. Today we look back at the 1960s and wonder
why we were all being told how to build nuclear fallout shelters.
Tomorrow we may look back on how things are in the world today, and
wonder why we were so afraid of the things that currently fill us with
dread. But fear moves on with us. Tomorrow there will be something else
to be afraid of, for sure.

So is it perhaps the case that the things we fear are not, in themselves,
the root of the problem?

The real serial killer is fear itself.

It is a killer because it is the one thing that, ultimately, can undermine love. The Guide warns us that 'perfect love eliminates fear', but it is tragically also true that deep fear blocks the flow of love.

And it is a serial killer, because it comes back at us in every generation wearing a different face. It even comes back at us in our own personal lives wearing many different faces. We think we have overcome one manifestation of our fears, and another one is lurking around the next corner.

Only fear can send us scuttling back to the lower brain reactions, and stop us striving for better, more imaginative and life-giving solutions to our problems. Only fear can put the brakes on our quest to become more fully human. Fear is the one enemy that can derail our journey towards the fullness of our humanity, and consign us back to the 'reptilian brain' of survival and defence.

If we could conquer fear, would we have overcome one of the biggest obstacles on the road to becoming fully human? There is reason to believe that our Guide thought so, because he is reported to have said '*Do not be afraid*' more times than most of us can count. And even more disturbing, the records say he called upon us to '*love our enemies*'. It seems that, according to the logic of Jesus, loving your enemies was a way of getting beyond the fear. Is this a case of hopeless idealism? Or is it a star we can steer our course by, even though we can never actually reach it? Is it, perhaps, even the Pole Star?

There is a story of a fearsome wolf that used to terrorise a village. At first the villagers ignored it, but after two or three fatal attacks, they became more and more defensive, but they couldn't decide how to deal with the problem of the wolf. Some of them said, 'We must go out there and kill the wolf.' Others said, 'We must build such a high fence around our village that nothing will ever be able to harm us.' Eventually they went to consult the Wise Man of the Woods who lived nearby. He listened to their story and then gave them his advice: 'Go home, and feed the wolf.'

The villagers were shocked and angered by this advice, and at first refused to act upon it. But gradually one or two brave souls started to put out food for the wolf, food that was eagerly taken. Soon the village had become used to the wolf, and the wolf had become almost tame. No longer driven by its raging hunger, it ceased to be a threat. But to get to the point of actually 'feeding the wolf', the villagers had to ally themselves with fear's opposite twin, 'trust'. They had to trust themselves and the wolf enough to make that first tentative contact. And they had to open their minds and their imaginations enough to understand the reasons for the wolf's attacks, and then try to address the underlying problem – the wolf's hunger.

Of course, life isn't as simple as this story might suggest. Even so, it is often true that when we befriend our fears, they turn out to be less fearsome than we thought. It has been wisely said that what we most acutely fear may actually be a blessing if we can face it and befriend it. It may be the greatest catalyst for growth that we have.

Unmask the murderer ...

In the summer of 2005 there was a big religious gathering of many thousands of pilgrims in Iraq. They were gathered there to pray, and to deepen their spiritual quest. They did not come together with any malice in their hearts. They meant each other no harm.

Then one day a rumour began to circulate through the teeming crowds of men, women and children. '*There may be a suicide bomber among us*' ...

Wherever this rumour was voiced, panic broke out. The people fled in fear. A stampede ensued. Over two thousand people were trampled to death, many of them women and children, the very old or the very young, the most vulnerable.

Who killed these people?

It wasn't the foreign armies occupying their land ... It wasn't an insurgent from among their own people ... It wasn't a suicide bomber. There *was* no suicide bomber!

Two thousand innocent people were killed by the *rumour* of a suicide bomber.

Two thousand people were killed *by fear alone*.

Such is the power of this notorious mass murderer, who doesn't even necessarily need human hands to help him!

Can you see evidence of 'the serial killer' at work in your life, especially in your personal and spiritual life?

How do you feel about the wolf story? Does it give us any guidance on how to deal with the 'climate of fear' that stalks our world today?

When fear becomes endemic, it can actually cause changes in the neural composition of our brains. It can make us 'set' in the 'lower brain mentality'. Do you see any evidence of this happening in our world today? If so, is there anything we can, and should do to counteract it?

What do you think would be the wisdom of our Guide on the subject? Try reading his story, to find the clues.

But there is another twist to the tale. Our fears are not merely a problem we have to deal with personally. They also put enormous power into the hands of those who have a vested interest in *controlling* us. And this brings us to the question of 'inner freedom' ...

Flying free?

Fear locks us into defensive positions that can actually cripple us and completely rob us of our freedom. And 'wings' are all about freedom. But what do we mean by freedom?

There is 'outer freedom' and there is 'inner freedom'. Outer freedom is constantly making its needs known. We know that it is right to stand up for the freedom of the oppressed, for example. Much blood has been spilled in the cause of national freedom, and human rights such as freedom of speech. At a personal level, we expect those around us to respect our need of a degree of freedom in our choices and actions. The ultimate deterrent against crime in most Western democracies is the withdrawal of freedom.

Suppose we had all these rights and freedoms, so that there was nothing left to campaign for. Would we then also have 'inner freedom'? I suspect not, because I have known people who are 'locked up', either in prison, or in the captivity of incapacitating illness, or loveless relationships or exploitative work situations, and yet they have had an inner freedom that I, frankly, envied. And I know many people who have every outward freedom they desire, and yet remain chained to their own fears and desires.

What prevents us from being inwardly free? The two culprits will not come as a surprise to you, in the light of all that we have been exploring. They were there on the savannah, and they are still here today. They masquerade as:

- Anything I inordinately hope to gain.
- Anything I inordinately fear to lose.

Faced with a choice about anything at all, I can only make that choice in a way that reflects the true core of my being, if I am not being pulled out of alignment with this true core, either by hope of gain or fear of loss. At the level of national politics we can see how true this is. How many of our important political decisions are truly made without hope of gain or fear of loss? It's easy to see how this dynamic operates in others, but what about ourselves?

The Guide told us '*The truth will set you free*'. To the extent that we can learn to make our choices and decisions in perfect balance with the true core of our being, unswayed by hope of gain or fear of loss, we will be truly free.

Take a little time to reflect on any choice you are pondering right now.
Which way does your true self want to choose?
Imagine your heart as a kind of pendulum, that can be swung two ways. One way is the 'hope of gain'. The other way is the 'fear of loss'. When you are being totally true to yourself, the pendulum rests in perfect balance.
Are you afraid of losing something in this matter? If so, name it to yourself and notice its power over you.
Are you hoping to gain something here? If so, notice what it is and why it is influencing you so much.
How is the pendulum behaving, as you make your choice?

We noticed, too, that our fears (but also our desire of gain) not only distort our choices in life, but also put power into the hands of others who have an interest in controlling us. Have you ever stopped to think how individual people or organisations (not excluding ecclesiastical organisations), or governments gain control over us? Or rather, what is it that makes us surrender something of our freedom to others?

An enlightening series on UK television (*The Power of Nightmare*), explored this very question. It was suggested that those who, for their own reasons, would persuade us to surrender some power to them often begin by promising us something really good, something we deeply desire, on condition that we give them our vote, and with that some of our freedom: 'Throw your lot in with me, and I will give you the glittering prizes'. The prizes may be anything from the best education system, the finest health care programme, a guaranteed minimum wage, or even a good feel about our spiritual status.

But in our jaded times, the population is no longer easily convinced that these prizes will be forthcoming, if they place their vote with the right party. Indeed, we have come to realise that not only is no one, of any party, going to deliver the goods, but in fact that no one ever *could* deliver the goods. We are being promised (at election time) a Utopia that can never exist. We have, understandably, become cynical about the promises and those who make them.

And so, it was suggested, the governance of many democratic countries has become less a matter of real power, and more a matter of administration and management, and this is not what satisfies those individuals who *really* want power, perhaps more than they desire the good of the electorate.

While many people in leadership roles serve the people faithfully and with integrity, there are also those who look for some other way to achieve the power they crave. 'If they won't buy into our *promises*,' we might hear them thinking, 'then let's try a different tack. Let's build up their *fears*, and then tell them we can *protect* them from what they most fear. If they won't buy the dream, let's sell them the nightmare and then offer to rescue them from it.' At a global level, the 'nightmare' might be another nation's 'weapons of mass destruction' (real or imagined), or the spread of bird flu or mass unemployment. At a personal level, the 'nightmare' that keeps us in check might be fear of exclusion from the 'group', or even the threat of exclusion from God's favour.

The Guide says '*Do not be afraid*'.

Anything that draws its power from our fears is not inspired or guided by *him*.

His vision is of a truth that sets us free.

He was crucified for unmasking the lies that hold us in thrall.

Where in our world today do you see the spread of fear?
What is fuelling it?
Who stands to gain from it?
Who is acquiring the control that you are surrendering?
How are they exercising that control – for their own gain, or for the greater good?
Is anyone 'selling us a nightmare'?

But our flight is beginning to look like an aerial battle between love and fear. Let's take a look at other aspects of being airborne – gentler patterns. Let's take a lesson from the birds, and learn to soar on the thermal currents and discover the great energy to be found in deep stillness …

Riding the thermals

Imagine a hillside on a warm, sunny afternoon. The air is calm and overhead the ravens are in flight. At least, their wings are spread, and they are in gentle motion, but actually they are doing nothing at all, and expending very little energy. They are letting themselves be carried on the thermal currents. Or imagine the same hillside on a stormy November morning. The winds are high, and those same ravens are surfing the skies, using the now overwhelmingly powerful currents to carry them along, still conserving their energy as best they can, and trusting that in the end they will arrive where they need to be.

The air isn't always calm around us either in the natural world or on our spiritual journey. We have seen something of the turbulence that, for example, fear can cause. But the invisible currents that will raise us up are always there for us, whatever the weather, if we know how to find them.

The Guide left us a parting gift:

'Peace I leave you,' he said, 'my peace I give you.'

Where might we find such peace?

In most modern languages the word 'peace' implies simply the absence of conflict. The peace of which the Guide speaks is something much more than this. It isn't a haven where there is no conflict. It is a dimension of reality that draws us to a level of our being that lies deeper, or higher, than the conflict, and where our savage differences can begin to be transcended. It is the kind of deep peace and surrender to the wholeness of things that, perhaps, we see in the birds who ride the thermals.

Words from the war poet, Wilfrid Owen, adapted for Benjamin Britten's *War Requiem* speak of 'wells we sunk too deep for war'. These 'wells' are also spaces of deep peace. They are the sacred space where enemies look into each other's eyes and see a human being looking back at them. There alone we can discover a power that can counter our fears and distrust, and free us to live, and to make our life's choices, from a higher place than the reptilian brain.

This is the peace of wholeness, expressed by the Hebrew word 'Shalom'. It can carry us beyond ourselves, and towards each other, as the thermals carry those ravens – a place where peace and power work together and bring us closer to the heart of life.

The Guide frequently went to his own 'deep wells', or 'rode the thermals', by taking time alone, in the hills, the desert, or in the calm of a friend's home. He urges us to visit the oases of stillness and depth in our lives, and when we pray, whatever prayer means for us, to do so in the still and secret centre of our hearts, not with a torrent of words.

The birds know instinctively where to find the currents that carry them upwards without any effort of their own. We are rather far removed from these foundational instincts, but even so there are ways in which we can 'ride the thermals' for ourselves, allowing the peace-power of Shalom to carry us. See whether any of these possibilities resonate with you …

Meditation, stillness, time simply to 'be', to do nothing at all and to do it with joy
A perceptive friend of mine once told me she pictured me as a bareback rider, standing on the back of a wild steed, holding its reins, but also holding the reins of several other horses that were also running wild, and trying, unsuccessfully to keep everything on an even keel. There was a lot of truth in what she said. Sometimes it feels very much like that, whether the other wild horses are difficult colleagues, demanding relatives, or simply tricky situations.

When life feels like this, one way I can find deeper 'shalom-space' is by practising some form of meditation, either formally, using tried and tested methods, or simply by seeking out a quiet spot, relaxing into a few minutes of silence and solitude, and letting myself be held in the arms of a mystery infinitely greater, stronger and wiser than I am. This brings a certain calm to the wild horses, and gives me space to reflect on which ones I really need to steer, and which I can, and should, allow to run their own courses.

The created world
There is a place of deep stillness that is always there, however your heart is feeling, and that is the great outdoors. Not that it is always calm there, of course, but even in her wildest moods, the natural world has the power to draw us beyond ourselves and touch the bedrock of our being. A brisk walk or a lingering stroll can restore a true perspective on the events of a troubled day. Five minutes on the park bench, watching the ripples on the lake or the flight of the clouds, or simple acts such as filling up the bird feeder and watching the customers fly in remind us that we are part of something much bigger than ourselves and enfold us once more into our ancient roots.

The creating world
Wherever and however human beings exercise their creativity, barriers dissolve. Music, for example, knows no boundaries. The same is true of

art, of sculpture, and of all fine craftsmanship. Drama, poetry, or a good novel or film take us to new depths of ourselves by engaging our highest emotions, challenging us to profound empathy, or simply strumming the hidden strings of our hearts until they seem to be beating in resonance with the universe. What another person has created opens up a 'well' within us. What we ourselves create, with our heads and our hands, nourishes our own hearts and the hearts of many others with living water.

'Spiritual conversations'

You might shudder at the very idea of a 'spiritual conversation'. Yet they go on all the time. Whenever two or more are gathered together to speak of things they hold dear and that give their lives meaning, then a spiritual conversation is taking place.

Traditionally the 'answers' to our questions about life's meaning have been handed down to us from on high, through the channels of a formal faith tradition. Today the growth of spiritual awareness, the ongoing quest that goes back to the cave paintings and the pyramids, is advancing more through conversations between people who are simply trying to discover, individually and together, what it means to become more fully human, in the model of the Guide.

These conversations are not about mental gymnastics, seeking to 'prove' something, but about the exchange of ideas and experience. They can happen at the pub, outside the school gates, over a coffee, or even over the internet, wherever two or more are gathered. Every conversation is part of the ripening process of our human-ness.

It's worth remembering the old adage, that when two people each have an apple, and then exchange those apples, each person still only has one apple. But if two people each have an idea, and they exchange those ideas, then each person has two ideas.

Shared celebration and ritual

When planet Earth crossed the threshold of the new millennium, we witnessed the first ever global celebration of life, accessible to most of the world's peoples through global television. Something very special happens when we come together in large numbers, or in smaller, more intimate gatherings, to celebrate, or to engage in shared rituals. In acting out our response to our human experience in this way, we deepen it, and in some way each participant shares in the energy flowing through all of us. We become, as a human family or a local community much more than the sum of our parts.

Not for nothing have the rites of passage we all share, such as birth, puberty, marriage and death, been ritualised in all human cultures to invite us, at crucial times, to enter the deeper layers of the invisible web of life to which we all belong and where we might recognise each other as brothers and sisters.

Story-telling, story-sharing, and deep listening

A picture is worth a thousand words, and a story is worth a thousand doctrines. Images and stories touch us at a much deeper level than mere words or instructions or admonitions. The Guide continually used stories to teach people more about who they were and who they could become. And these stories were full of pictures.

In our day, the quest for what it means to be fully human is much more likely to advance through the sharing of our stories, and this in turn requires us to become good listeners. Everyone has a story. When we reflect on the story of our own experience, we discover our personal wisdom. When we listen with an open heart and genuine interest to another's story, then the wisdom that person has garnered from their experience will be shared with us, and we will both grow in the process.

Being open to authentic encounters with others, especially with those who are not like us

We tend to do most of our inner growing when we are forced out of our comfort zones. This usually means dealing with people or situations that provoke our dislike or disagreement or even our fear. It has been wisely said that there are at least two levels of 'truth'. At one level, the opposite of a true statement is a false statement. At a deeper level, the opposite of a true statement can be another true statement. One of the hardest challenges of becoming more fully human is to listen with respect to opinions that are at variance with our own, to really hear and reflect upon constructive criticism that comes our way, and to acknowledge that our opponents and critics also carry a strand of the divine mystery in their hearts. This awareness is a deep and threatening space to enter, but there may be unexpected treasure in its depths. It may become the source of a deeper peace and understanding.

Letting our suffering stretch our hearts

The deepest, darkest 'well' of all is the experience of suffering. Our own suffering is bad enough, but even worse is when we have to be helplessly present to the suffering of others, especially those we love. With our heads we can tell ourselves that we suffer because we are still in the throes of our growing into all we shall become, and growth is always painful. But in our gut and in our hearts, suffering makes no sense. It gouges out great

caverns within us. Yet it is precisely these gaping holes of pain and emptiness inside us that can become pools of grace and wisdom. They can
stretch our hearts.

Perhaps you are aware of craters like this in your own heart? The
wisdom and grace that gathers in these craters can become living water
for others, who will quite possibly drink courage and compassion from
your well without ever knowing, or needing to know, what caused the
emptiness inside you that made the space for it. And if becoming more
fully human is about the growth and evolution of the heart, then this
painful shaping and stretching may be a crucial element of the process.

What helps you to find the 'peace that passes understanding'?
Where are those elusive thermal currents for you?
Where are the wells that lie deeper than the conflict zones in your life?
Are you drinking from them as often as you need to?

Over the edge

One of my most vivid images – part-dream, part-prayer, is of a wide and raging river. Imagine yourself standing on the banks of such a river. And imagine that you know, beyond doubt, that you have to cross it – that it is imperative that you reach the far side.

Perhaps humanity is standing, even now, on the banks of this river. Perhaps we have come as far as we can and our future destiny beckons us from the distant bank. To plunge into the river seems like certain death. And yet to stay 'on the safe side' is to stagnate and eventually to die. Are we standing between a rock and a hard place? Is there any way forward that doesn't lead us into disaster? These are not just interesting existential questions. They are an expression of how many of us are actually feeling in today's world with its seemingly impossible choices and unmanageable conflicts.

One of the Guide's paradoxical sayings was this:

'Anyone who loses his life shall find it.'

If we are willing to risk losing our lives, we will find them. If we try to hang on to what we have, we will lose it. Let's listen to his wisdom as we stand on the river bank.

The image, for me, moved on. One day there appeared a single, but solid, stepping stone, brought to me by a stranger who seemed to mean well with me. In faith I stepped out onto this stone, into the river. There was just one stone, and I had to wait and trust that another would arrive. Day by day the stranger brought more stepping stones, but only one at a time, and always with a waiting time in between. And each time I stepped onto the next stone, I was actually stepping out further into the fast-running currents of the river, further away from the safety of the riverbank, and with no guarantee that there would indeed be another stone, and another, until I arrived at the distant shore. But I had begun to trust the bringer of the stones.

One day he was late. I turned round to see what might be delaying him. And then I saw where he was getting the stepping stones from. He was taking apart my nice comfortable cottage on the shore, to provide me with the means to cross to the other side. Truly, now, there was no way back. Yesterday was being surrendered in order to create Tomorrow.

The Guide warns us to expect shocks like this, and to be ready to let go of what we thought was all sewn up. Nothing we can imagine is ever going to be the final word on anything. We have to make this crossing in trust. And this is one of the hallmarks of the spiritual journey, when it goes beyond conventional religious practice. It is no longer a matter of believing a set of declared or revealed truths, set down in doctrinal statements. It has become a question of trust. 'Faith' moves beyond believing into trusting. Trust is the only bridge we have across the troubled waters of Today, and the Guide tells us to proceed on trust.

'Your faith will make you whole.'

When Jesus speaks words like these to the sick and the lost and the troubled, he isn't saying, 'Go to church every Sunday and recite the creed'. He is saying, 'If you *trust* in the power of my presence, you will come through.'

But the stepping stone story also reminds us that everything is built on, and evolves out of, what has gone before. If you remember our journey, earlier in this book, through the aeons of evolution, you will recall that all life grows out of previous layers of existence. Recall how our brains have evolved, each new improved 'model' being an additional layer over what went before. The Guide also says:

'I haven't come to abolish what has gone before, but to fulfil it.'

That fulfilment, however, may require us to shed anything that is no longer helping us to become more human. It's not a matter of rebellion or rejection. It's a matter of *growth*. The Guide goes on to suggest that '*new wine should be put into new wineskins*'. To try to put new wine into old wineskins will cause the old skins to burst and the wine to be lost. Retaining a right relationship between respecting and building on all that has gone before, and at the same time risking the 'new wineskins' is one of the delicate balancing skills we need to learn as we take to our wings.

Some creatures carry their skeletons on the outside of their bodies. When they grow out of them, they have to shed the whole skeleton and grow a new, bigger one. The new one won't be something completely different. It will look like the old one, but it will fit. However, there is a time gap between shedding the old skeleton and growing the new, when the creature has no external armour at all. It has literally lost the structure that was holding it together. During this period it is very vulnerable, and exposed to all kinds of predators. It has lost an outgrown layer of protection in order to grow a new layer of security that fits its new size and shape.

It seems that the human family is in that kind of place right now. We have grown out of much of what we thought was so definite and absolute, in terms of some of our former religious 'certainties' and solid social structures. We have had to shed them; otherwise we would have suffocated and died. But the new layer of understanding that we need, to deal with where we find ourselves hasn't grown yet. We are extremely vulnerable.

Some of us react to this feeling of vulnerability and exposure by building up more defences, becoming more dogmatic and exclusive, and trying to tighten, rather than relax the reins. Religious fundamentalism is an example of this attempt to reinforce securities that no longer hold.

Others react by plunging into the ocean of uncertainty, and 'trying on', indiscriminately, any and every new 'answer' that presents itself. New Age spirituality can be at risk of going to this extreme.

The way between these two extremes is to use discernment in finding our way forward across the troubled waters of uncertainty. This way invites us to take the risk of Tomorrow, and not to try to fossilise ourselves into past structures that may have served us well, but are no longer leading us to life. But we also need to look where we are going, and reflect on what is truly leading to life, and what may be militating against the quest for our full humanity. We can then, as we have already seen, actively nourish the former, and work against the latter.

Meanwhile, we stand on the riverbank and ask ourselves:

Should we cross in trust, or hold on to our stronghold on this side of the river?
Which do we desire more: the established riverside cottage, or the stepping stones?
We can't have both: the stones of the cottage are needed to create the path across the river.
What do you feel? What does the river mean to you? What specific threshold lies before you?
Would the crossing of this threshold help you to become more fully alive, more truly the person you are destined to be?
Is anything holding you back?

When the fledgling bird stands on the edge of the nest, it is not peering into the abyss where all is lost, but over the threshold that beckons it towards the next phase of its life.

The fact is that there is no edge to our 'becoming human'. The edge we fear to cross is no more real than the horizon of our present vision. The idea into which the Guide calls us has no limits. Perhaps our fears are so great only because our vision is so small, and trust is the only bridge that will lead us across this chasm.

Oscars and red cards

Where is the spiritual quest to become human going in the twenty-first century?

Where are the signs of growth, and where are the dark zones that are pulling us back from our quest to become more and more fully human?

Suppose you were invited to award Oscars for areas of our lives that are helping to make us *more human*, and to hand out red penalty cards for areas that are tending to *dehumanise* us. What would you select?

My own Oscar list would include things like:

- Organisations that are truly working for the greater good of humankind, including most of the charity organisations and their workers and all who support them with practical or financial help.
- Everyone who is working for an increase in justice in a grossly unfair world, whether in a large and visible organisation, or in one of the very many little gatherings, world-wide, of a few committed individuals who quietly get on with the job of bringing justice into their own communities.
- Investigative journalism that exposes injustice and corruption on a scale we have never known before, and all those who live true to their own integrity in situations that put their jobs, and even their lives at risk. And the photographers and film-makers who make us look full-on at the anguish, the hunger, and the violence going on around us, and taking away our excuse that 'we didn't know'.
- Everyone who cares about our living planet, whether they are on the forefront of environmental research, or in a position to make decisions about funding, or whether they simply faithfully recycle their cans and bottles each week.
- People who make space in a crazy world for stillness, for themselves and for others; people who open up small oases in our cities where people can drop in for a moment's quiet; people who are prepared to *listen* to the stories of others.
- Anything that forces us to use our imaginations, to leave our comfort zones, and to 'think outside the box'. Usually this means circumstances and challenges we would have tried to avoid if we had seen them coming.
- People who make peace, whether in international politics, in the work-

place, in the home or in the school playground. Everyone who defuses a squabble helps to prevent a war.

- Global television, and the internet (at their *best* – at their worst they would get the red card!), for revealing to us that we are indeed one human family, living on a very small planet, and that we can be inter-connected, at the click of a mouse, to each other and to the world.
- Everyone who protests when their leaders take unjust or inhuman courses of action. Everyone who ever says 'There is a better way'. Everyone who adds their voice to the universal cry for peaceful solutions to the world's conflicts, and refuses to take 'no' for an answer.
- Everyone who adds a spark of new life to life: by bringing up a child; by singing a song; by creating something new, whether it is a tasty meal or a work of art, or simply by giving a word of encouragement or a friendly smile on a rainy day.
- Everyone who makes a 'decision to love' – to care for the sick or the dying, the disabled or the marginalised, the unlovable and the unlovely. If enough of us could really do this, even occasionally, then there would be no one in the world uncared for.

And where would my red cards go? What would I like to send off the pitch? What is tending to *de*humanise us?

- Whatever tends to fundamentalism and seeks to lock us into false 'securities', telling us that our way is the only way and therefore all other ways must be wrong.
- Whatever encourages us to focus on our image and our 'fig leaves' instead of trusting the truth of who we, and others, really are. Anything that tells us 'we are not worth anything' until and unless we put on our 'masks'.
- Man-made rules that claim to have been delivered by 'God'.
- Whatever deliberately fuels our fears, especially if it then claims to protect us from them.
- Labels that we pin on each other, and on ourselves, and pigeon-holes in which we place each other, because these are the raw ingredients of exclusion, and the dream of humanity is all-inclusive.
- Hierarchies of power, whether political, social, economic or religious, if they run on an agenda of keeping the majority of people helpless, impotent, infantile and 'under control'.
- Whatever claims to satisfy our superficial wants and wishes, but leaves our hearts to starve – junk food, whether it is pumped into our bodies, our minds or our souls, or all three, and everyone who makes a profit from trivialising what it means to be Human. Every form of 'dumbing down'.

- Whatever undermines our trust in each other and in life, whether in high profile, dramatic betrayals by secular or religious leaders, or in everyday situations that poison the wells of truth in an infinite variety of ways.
- The dark side of television and the media that encourage us to look on at the lives of others, instead of being active participants in life, and especially anything that fosters the lower brain reactions by inviting us to vote off those who 'fail' and to gloat over the humiliation of those we choose to designate the losers.

So! I feel better for that! What about you? Where will *your* Oscars go, and what provokes your red cards?

But the purpose of the exercise is not to wallow in our own pet gripes, but to seriously consider, together, what in our world today is making us more human, and what is tending to *dehumanise* us. What do *you* think? You might find it fruitful to share your reflections with a group of friends.

Kneeprints in the sand

The phrase 'one small step for man, one giant leap for [hu]mankind' has become a cliché.

When the first human being set foot on the moon, it was just such a small step and huge leap. But there have been even smaller steps and bigger leaps.

The story we have traced in these pages has been punctuated by footprints. In the beginning the wisdom of the universe left its prints in the stardust that would give rise, over aeons of evolution, to you and me. We are specks of stardust. We are also sparks of God.

As life began to move towards human form, it left its prints in the volcanic mud of Tanzania, announcing that we had become bipedal.

Two thousand years ago another set of prints marked the desperate trail of a young family fleeing from terror in Palestine to the relative safety of Egypt. The prints of the child would become markers for the whole human family to plot a true course towards becoming fully human.

Through the centuries since then, the narrow way to transcendence reveals the prints of millions of searchers, who follow a dream, and, in following, help to make it a reality. Your footprints and mine are in there too, sometimes so heavy that we can barely move, sometimes so light that we could almost fly. It all depends on how much we try to carry with us.

In the sixth century an Irish sailor, who would become known as St Brendan the Navigator, also left some prints behind in the sands of time, and, more precisely, on an Irish beach, as he knelt to ask God's blessing on all that might lie ahead, climbed into a fragile little coracle, and entrusted himself to an unpredictable sea and an unimaginable destination.

One small step for Brendan, a final prayer on his native soil, but it was the step that first brought the wisdom of our Guide, and the vision of a new Way, to the British Isles and beyond.

To make that small step, Brendan had to step right 'outside the box', and trust in a process that seemed to fly in the face of common sense and the instinct to stay safe.

Perhaps humankind stands on the brink of a similar kind of creative discontinuity today. Perhaps one day it will even become apparent that the evolutionary edge, which has until now appeared to be about the survival of the fittest, may in the future lie in learning the art of co-operation, rather than competition and of working for the greater good of all creation rather than defending our own corner.

There are indications that this movement towards new directions in the evolutionary story is already beginning to reveal itself. Look at your Oscar list for some real examples.

One small step is all any of us can make, but that one small step can become an essential part of the great leap of humankind beyond the present limitations of *homo sapiens* … Or not? – The choice is ours.

We can trudge on along life's way, having regard mainly for our own well-being. Or we can pause, like Brendan, to reflect on the greater vision that draws us forward, and leave our own kneeprints in the sand …

… as a continuing invocation to the deep and loving wisdom of the universe to guide our flight into all that humankind can become,

… as an expression of trust that is stronger than all our fears, and longs for the courage to step into the coracle of the still-unknown and unexplored, and say Yes! to the Mystery,

… and with a heart overflowing with gratitude to the unquenchable power and mysterious source of life that gives us …

roots and wings.

Some interesting books . . .

Armstrong, Karen, *A History of God* (London: Vintage, 1999).

Berry, Thomas and Swimme, Brian, *The Universe Story* (HarperSanFrancisco, 1994).

Brody, Hugh, *The Other Side of Eden: Hunter Gatherers, Farmers and the Shaping of the World* (London: Faber and Faber, 2001).

Bryson, Bill, *A Short History of Nearly Everything* (London: Black Swan, 2004).

Campbell, Joseph, *The Hero with a Thousand Faces* (London: Fontana Press, 1993).

Capra, Fritjof, *The Web of Life* (London: Flamingo, 1997).

Chief Seathl, *Chief Seathl's Testament* (Coalville, Leics: Saint Bernard Press, 1994).

Chilton Pearce, Joseph, *The Biology of Transcendence* (Rochester, Vermont: Park Street Press, 2002).

Dalai Lama, His Holiness the, *The Universe in a Single Atom* (London: Little, Brown, 2005).

Davies, Paul, *God and the New Physics* (London: Penguin Books, 1983).

Davies, Paul, *The Mind of God* (London: Penguin Books, 1992).

Dawkins, Richard, *The Selfish Gene* (Oxford University Press, 1976).

—*The Ancestor's Tale* (London: Phoenix, 2005).

Dossey, Larry, *Recovering the Soul* (London: Bantam, 1989).

Douglas-Klotz, Neil, *The Hidden Gospel: Decoding the Spiritual Message of the Aramaic Jesus* (Wheaton, Illinois: Quest Books, 1999).

Fernandez-Armesto, Felipe, *So You Think You're Human?* (Oxford University Press, 2004).

Fox, Matthew, *Creation Spirituality* (HarperSanFrancisco, 1991).

Fripp, Robert, *Let There Be Life* (New Jersey: Hidden Spring, 2001).

Greenfield, Susan, *The Human Brain – A Guided Tour* (London: Weidenfeld and Nicolson, 1997).

Hughes, Gerard W., *God of Surprises* (Darton, Longman and Todd, 1985).

Jones, Steven, *In the blood – God, Genes and Destiny* (London: Flamingo, 1997).

Kuhn, Thomas S., *The Structure of Scientific Revolutions* (The University of Chicago Press, 1962).

Kumar, Satish, *You Are, Therefore I Am* (Dartington: Green Books, 2002).

Leakey, Richard and Lewin, Roger, *Origins Reconsidered* (London: Abacus, 1993).

Lovelock, James, *Gaia* (Oxford University Press, 1979).

Lynch, John and Barrett, Louise, *Walking with Cavemen* (London: Headline, 2002, by arrangement with the BBC).

Mithen, Steven, *The Prehistory of the Mind* (London: Phoenix, 1996)

Margulis, Lynn and Sagan, Dorion, *What Is Life?* (New York: Simon and Schuster, 1995).

McGrath, Alister, *Dawkins' God* (Oxford: Blackwell Publishing, 2005).

Nelson, Rabbi David W., *Judaism, Physics and God* (Woodstock, Vermont: Jewish Lights Publishing, 2005).

O'Murchu, Diarmuid, *Evolutionary Faith* (Maryknoll, New York: Orbis Books, 2002).

Oppenheimer, Stephen, *Out of Eden – The Peopling of the World* (London: Constable, 2003).

Peck, M. Scott, *The Road Less Travelled* (London: Arrow Books, 1983).

Quinn, Daniel, *Beyond Civilisation*, (New York: Three Rivers Press, 1999).

Rees, Martin, *Our Cosmic Habitat* (London: Phoenix, 2003).

—*Just Six Numbers* (London: Weidenfeld and Nicolson, 1999).

Rilke, Rainer Maria, *Selected Poems*, translated by J. B. Leishman (London: Penguin, 2005).

Rohr, Richard, *Everything Belongs* (New York: Crossroad, 1999).

Rupp, Joyce, *The Cosmic Dance* (Maryknoll, New York: Orbis Books, 2002).

Sagan, Carl, *Cosmos* (London: Abacus, 1995).

Schroeder, Gerald L., *The Hidden Face of God* (New York: The Free Press, 2001).

Smith, Adrian B., *The God Shift* (The Liffey Press, Dublin, 2004)

Spong, John Selby, *A New Christianity for a New World* (HarperSanFrancisco, 2001)

Southgate, Dr Christopher (ed.), *God, Humanity and the Cosmos* (London/New York: T and T. Clark, 1999).

Southwood, Richard, *The Story of Life* (Oxford University Press, 2003).

Soyinka, Wole, *Climate of Fear: The BBC Reith Lectures* (London: Profile Press, 2004).

Sykes, Bryan, *The Seven Daughters of Eve* (London: Corgi Books, 2001).

Tacey, David, *The Spirituality Revolution* (Hove: Brunner-Routledge, 2004).

Teilhard de Chardin, Pierre, *The Phenomenon of Man* (London: Fontana, 1965).

—*The Prayer of the Universe* (London: Fontana, 1973).

—*The Future of Man* (New York: Image Books, Doubleday, 2004, first published Paris: Editions de Seuil, 1959).

Ward, Keith, *God – A Guide for the Perplexed* (Oxford: Oneworld Publications, 2003).

Wheatley, Margaret J., *Leadership and the New Science* (San Francisco: Berrett-Koehler Publishers Inc., 1999).

—*Turning to One Another* (San Francisco: Berrett-Koehler Publishers Inc., 2002).

Winston, Robert, *The Human Mind* (London: Bantam, 2003).

—*Human Instinct* (London: Bantam, 2002).

Young, Jeremy, *The Cost of Certainty* (London: Darton, Longman and Todd, 2004).

Zimmer, Carl, *Evolution* (London: Arrow Books, 2003).